WOODBURNING
Realistic People

Pour Me a Drink by Jo Schwartz.

Step-by-Step Guide to Creating Perfect Portraits of People

WOODBURNING
—————— *Realistic People*

BY JO SCHWARTZ

FOX CHAPEL
PUBLISHING

Dedication

I would never have dabbled in the woodburning world had it not been for Ralph Dulaney, the webmaster of www.woodburner.com and a friend to all who burn throughout the world. Those shared photographs of so many techniques and styles sparked my interest, and the encouragement from friends I met on that website kept me striving to improve. Dumitru Muradian, who was originally from Bucharest, Romania, is still a close friend whom I've never met in person, but we have shared many burning tips over the years. (Mostly he shared, and I wrote as many notes as possible!) NL Cong is from Darwin, NT, Australia, and she spent many hours guiding me to "see" what I was burning. Last, but not least, thanks to my family and friends, who had to put up with those beginning trial and error burns and who all waited patiently for me to come into my own pyrography style.

ISBN 978-1-56523-880-0

Library of Congress Cataloging-in-Publication Data

Names: Schwartz, Jo, 1958- author.
Title: Woodburning realistic people / Jo Schwartz.
Description: East Petersburg : Fox Chapel Publishing, [2017] | Includes index.
Identifiers: LCCN 2016052862 | ISBN 9781565238800
Subjects: LCSH: Pyrography. | Portraits.
Classification: LCC TT199.8 .S39 2017 | DDC 745.51/4--dc23
LC record available at https://lccn.loc.gov/2016052862

To learn more about the other great books from Fox Chapel Publishing, or to find a retailer near you, call toll-free 800-457-9112 or visit us at *www.FoxChapelPublishing.com*.

Note to Authors: We are always looking for talented authors to write new books. Please send a brief letter describing your idea to Acquisition Editor, 1970 Broad Street, East Petersburg, PA 17520.

Printed in Singapore
First printing

Two Guns by Carlos Arturo Castellanos.

Contents

Introduction

Woodburning is probably one of the oldest forms of art, but it's not exactly mainstream, so people often wonder how I got started. Well, I don't draw, I can't paint, and I learned the hard way that I can't whittle, either! Whittling is what brought me to woodburning, though. I was playing around with an old burner, trying to "fix" a carved figure with no success ... but I did like the look of the burnt areas.

I went online to see if other people might like the same things and wandered onto the www.woodburning.com site. I was inspired by the variety of styles and subjects, and knew I wanted to try burning some trees and mountains. To this day, my mountains and trees are awful. On a whim, I tried to do a human portrait, never believing that I could do it because my trees were so bad. My portraits weren't great at first, but I knew almost instinctively what to do to achieve certain results, and my work improved.

Each burn was, and still is, a learning experience. I relied on the generosity of people I met online to answer questions about types of wood, burning machines, etc. These helpful souls also posted hundreds of photographs to look at for inspiration. Some of the photographs really caught my eye and I wanted to emulate their "look," but even with the artists' tips I had to work it out for myself.

My goal in writing this book is to share the techniques I have developed over the years to burn realistic human portraits. We'll start just like I did, with some inspirational photos that will show you different styles of burning portraits. We'll talk a little bit about tools, materials, and making patterns. Then, we'll dive into techniques. I'll divide the parts of the face into smaller sections and teach you how I recreate each feature on wood, and then I'll show you how to combine and vary those few techniques to create your own human portraits. And the same way my family and online friends encouraged me when I first started, I will encourage you and help you hone your skill as a pyrographer.

You don't need much to get started: a few small pieces of wood, a woodburner with an adjustable temperature control, a burning pen or nib, and a couple of other basic supplies. However, portraits can be tricky, and even though I will go slowly, it's best if you have some experience with woodburning. At the very least, turn on the machine and (carefully!) play with it for a few days. See page 21 for instructions to make sample boards,

This was my first piece, burned at the end of December 2004.

Here I am in my studio.

Other than a woodburning unit and some wood, you don't need much to start burning.

Precious Moments was inspired by a painting by the artist Fritz Zuber Buhler. Sometimes when I view paintings from the old masters, I "see" them in sepia and know they will make an excellent burn. The basswood burning is 12" by 12" and dates from 2011.

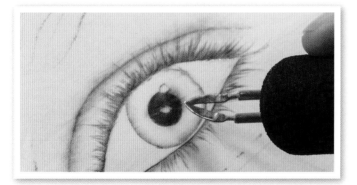

The lessons start with an eye and then build the face around it.

Marshal Hickok shows the reenactor who portrays the famous Abilene, Kan., marshal most weekends during the summer. The basswood burning is 12" by 12" and dates from 2010.

Pour Me A Drink shows a reenactor who plays different characters. The work is 12" by 14" and was burned on basswood in 2014.

which will help you get comfortable holding the pen and understand how the nib and heat interact with the wood.

The lessons start with an eye. You will learn how to do the eyelid crease, which is exactly how you shape a nose or make a wrinkle in skin, and is used again on lips and even to add shading between fingers or to round off a collar. The majority of samples are from photographs of real people I took with my little camera. (I basically told my family to line up, 'cause Momma needs some body parts!)

Pyrography is admittedly a slow art form. I burn in layers, building up the color a little at a time. It takes me several hours to do a nose. You can expect to spend two weeks or more working on a basic portrait, plus more time if you decide to fill in the background. But people really love the slightly old-fashioned sepia look of a woodburned portrait as well as the permanence of a wooden artwork. If you practice and are patient, you can make a beautiful treasure for your family.

Now, let's get started!

Chapter 1
GALLERY

Big John: Hippie Christ '95 by Dino Muradian of Mississauga, Ont., is 11¾" by 13" and burned on a maple panel.

These are some outstanding portraits by friends in the pyrography world. I hope they will give you an idea of what you can accomplish and inspire you to try a variety of burning styles, backgrounds, and materials in your portraits.

The Chief is by Adin Begich of Charlotte, N.C. It is 11" by 21¼" and burned in cherry.

Mother Love by David Kreider of Harrisonburg, Va., is a 12" by 20" woodburning on poplar.

Mother Theresa, 8" by 10", is by Alex Yawor of Aliquippa, Pa., and was burned in Baltic birch.

Butterfly Girls is by Steve Hawkes of Elwell, Mich., and was based on a photograph of four-year-old twin sisters.

Determined by Cate McCauley of West Greenwich, Conn., is 7" by 9" and burned on paper.

Abby by Minisa Robinson of Rifle, Colo., is 8" by 10" and burned on basswood.

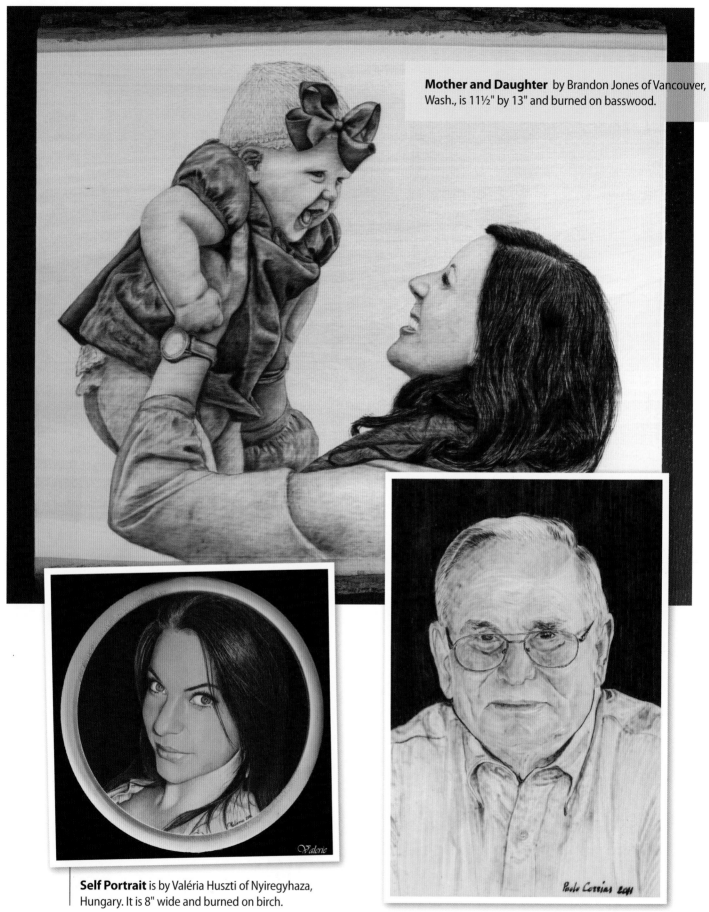

Mother and Daughter by Brandon Jones of Vancouver, Wash., is 11½" by 13" and burned on basswood.

Self Portrait is by Valéria Huszti of Nyiregyhaza, Hungary. It is 8" wide and burned on birch.

A Great Man—Albino Raffaele is by Paolo Corrias of Sinnai, Sardinia, Italy. It is 20cm by 30cm and burned on Italian poplar.

Black Woman is by Hubert Van de Sande of Brasschaat, Belgium. It is 20cm by 30cm and burned on birch plywood.

Forest Native by Mick Richards of Davenport Wash., 10½" by 44", was burned on ponderosa pine and accented with watercolor and colored pencil.

Two Guns is by Carlos Arturo Castellanos. It is 18" by 24" and made of Minnesota basswood.

Africa by Stefania Mante of Rome, Italy, is 7¾" by 11¾".

Chapter 2
GETTING STARTED

Michio by Fay Helfer of Brasschaat, Belgium, is an 11" by 14" pyrography on wood with pastel and natural pigments from red cabbage, pomegranate, and turmeric.

We're going to start with a few words on the tools and materials you'll need to get started, as well as the general techniques and safety habits you should practice before you get too far into the projects.

Tools

Woodburning is a great form of art for many reasons. One of them is that it doesn't take much equipment to get started. You need a woodburning unit and a few basic drafting tools that you probably have lying around the house, plus some wood.

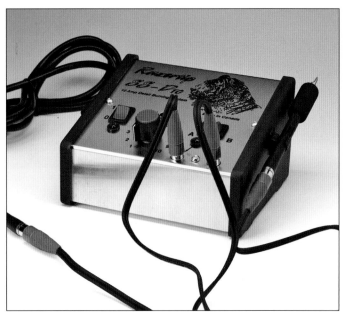

I use a Razertip SS-D10. However, any burner with adjustable heat will work fine.

THE WOODBURNING UNIT

First and foremost, you're going to need a woodburning unit. If you've been at this awhile, you probably have one. The burner model isn't critical; as long as it has adjustable heat and you are reasonably comfortable controlling it, it will probably work for these projects.

If you're curious, I use a Razertip SS-D10. It has interchangeable pens, rather than replaceable nibs (tips or points), and this particular model allows me to plug in two pens at a time. Several manufacturers, including Burnmaster, Colwood, Detail Master, and Optima, make similar or equivalent units; check with your local woodworking store or visit the manufacturers' websites for details. Walnut Hollow also makes a less expensive variable-temperature burner that is widely available at craft stores.

The Colwood Detailer can be used with fixed nib and replaceable nib pens.

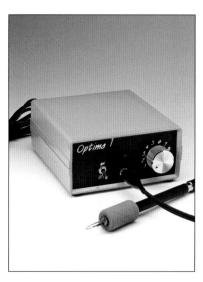

Optima's burners use either regular or heavy-duty interchangeable pens.

Walnut Hollow's Versa Tool is available at craft stores.

NIBS AND PENS

I use three Razertip pens daily: the Heavy Duty Medium Spear Shader, the Small Spear Shader, and the 1.5mm Ball tip. The spear shaders look like very small pie servers, while the Ball tip literally has a tiny ball at the end.

The most valuable and versatile pen for me is the Medium Spear Shader. You will need that pen tip or something similar to do the projects in this book. Almost every type of burning machine has a similar pen or nib. My smooth shading style can be accomplished with many different nibs; it is the way you use the tool that is important, not necessarily the actual nib or pen.

Note: The "nib" is the metal point that heats and touches the wood. The pen is the shaft that you hold. Some woodburning units have interchangeable nibs and others have interchangeable pens, which is why I'm using the words somewhat interchangeably here.

CLEANING THE NIBS

Because you are burning wood, carbon will build up on the nibs. Using a dirty or grimy tip will not only affect the smoothness of the stroke, but it can scratch the surface of the wood. We will be burning at lower heat temperatures, so there is less likelihood of the nibs becoming grimy. However, you should check and clean the nib regularly, especially before you begin the flesh areas of a portrait. If you accidently get a wood type that is sticky or sappy, or you touch the nib to something that melts, stop and clean the nib right away.

There are many ways to clean the delicate tips. I use aluminum oxide and a leather strop. It doesn't take much to keep the tip clean and smooth—I've only purchased one bottle of aluminum oxide in 10 years! Other pyrographers use sandpaper or steel wool; both make me shudder. I prefer to treat my pen tips gently.

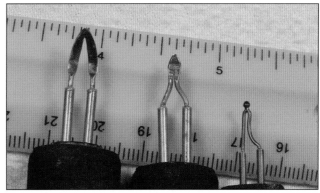

You need just three nibs: the Heavy Duty Medium Spear Shader, the Small Spear Shader, and the 1.5mm Ball tip.

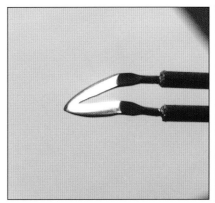 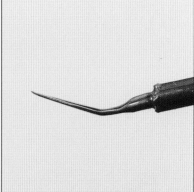

The spear shader is easy to identify; it looks like a tiny pie server.

With a dab of aluminum oxide and a leather strop, you can clean nibs in minutes.

To clean a nib, put a dab of aluminum oxide on a leather strop (the rough side of scrap leather). Let the nib cool, and then stroke it through the aluminum oxide and across the strop until it is bright and shiny. Wipe the tip on a clean cloth, and you're ready to burn again.

BUILDING A BURNING KIT

You'll need to gather a handful of household items to have on hand while you burn. You probably have all of these things lying around, so you just need to collect them in your work space.

- Light: Position it opposite your dominant hand so the shadow falls behind your hand, off the wood.
- Scrap of plywood or cardboard: Use it to protect the table.
- Fan: For pulling smoke away. See Safety on page 34.
- Sandpaper and sanding block or orbital sander or drum sander. To prepare the surface of the wood. See Wood Prep on page 25.
- Rag or tack cloth: To wipe the wood after sanding.
- Graphite paper: To transfer the pattern. See Transferring the Pattern to the Wood on page 47.
- Masking tape: To hold down the pattern while you trace it.
- Red or blue ballpoint pen: For tracing; the color shows up nicely against the black pattern lines.
- Pencil, pencil sharpener: For drawing any pattern lines you might have missed.
- Eraser (such as a white art eraser): For removing the pattern lines as you work.
- Needle-nose pliers (optional): For removing hot nibs from solid-point and interchangeable nib burners.
- Leather strop and aluminum oxide honing compound: To clean dirty nibs. See Cleaning the Nibs, page 19.
- Sharp blade (assorted): Razor blade, tip of knife, safety pin, etc. I keep an assortment of sharp things on hand for highlights, fine hairs, removing mistakes, and so much more.

MAKING SAMPLE BOARDS

Sample boards, which are also known as layer guides and value, or heat, guides, give you a chance to practice and get comfortable with your woodburning machine while you make useful tools. The boards will show the effect of each of your machine's heat settings on the different types of wood you will use for projects, as well as the effect of adding more layers of burning at a particular heat setting.

Taking the time to make sample boards now will speed up your decisions later. You'll be able to refer back to the setting for the value of darkness that you want to achieve in certain areas of your portraits. When in doubt always use a lower/cooler temperature and rely on layering to achieve the depth of darkness required.

You'll need three samples of your burning material, a pencil, a ruler, and your burning unit.

Make the Heat Sample

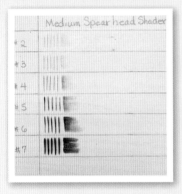

Make the Value Guide

Make the Layer Guide

Make the Heat Sample

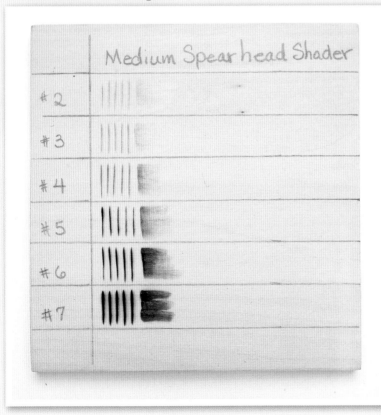

Step 1: Draw 10 rectangles on a piece of sample wood; number each space. (If your burner has fewer than 10 temperature settings, draw as many rectangles as you have settings.)

Step 2: Adjust the woodburning unit to its lowest setting. Draw some lines and do some shading in rectangle #1. Then, turn up the burner one level and repeat. Keep going until you scorch the wood. In my sample, the #7 heat setting is too hot; it scorched the wood. I would never use that setting, and there's no need to test the higher settings because they will also be too hot.

Make the Value Guide

Step 1: Draw 10 rectangles on a piece of sample wood; number each space.

Step 2: Burn #10 first, darkening it completely. Use the setting that darkened the scrap without scorching it, and burn slowly and deeply for this darkest square. Make a note of the heat setting and the number of layers you burn.

Step 3: Return to square #1 and adjust the unit to the its lowest setting. There should be almost no discernable color happening as you burn that square. For portraits you *must* have a #1 setting that produces very little to no color. You'll use this setting for highlights and burnishing.

Step 4: Barely turn the heat up and burn square #2. You want to layer this square a couple of times to get it to change from value #1. Note the heat setting and the values near the square.

Step 5: Repeat Step 4 to fill the rest of the squares. You should end up with a smooth gradation of color from basically nothing (white) to completely dark (black). Because the Heat Sample has fewer choices than the 10 squares in the Value Guide, you will have to layer the Value Guide squares to create the gradation.

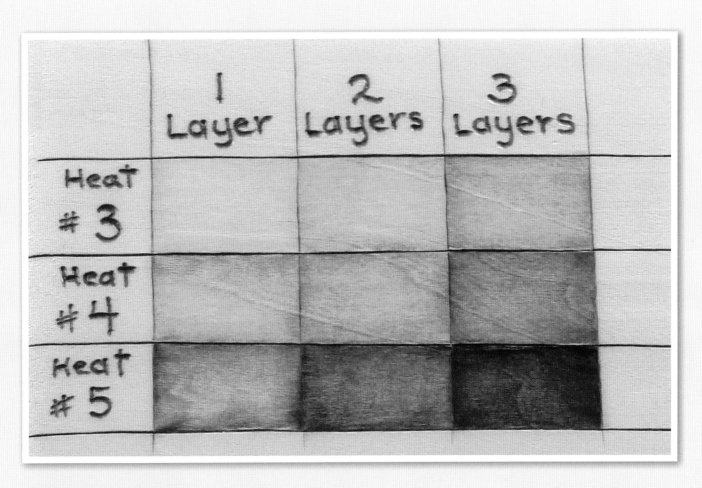

Make the Layer Guide

Step 1: Draw a grid on a piece of wood. Make it at least four columns wide by four columns tall. Label the layers and heat settings as shown.

Step 2: Adjust the burner to heat setting #3. Fill in all three squares in that row. Then, add one more layer of color to the "2 layers" square and two more layers to the "3 layers" square.

Step 3: Turn up the burner and repeat Step 2 for the remaining heat settings. Notice that you can use a lower heat setting and, by layering, still create darker values. This trick comes in handy when doing the edges of the face or jaw. You can maintain lighter skin tones and still get a deep, rich look.

Materials

I often burn on basswood, but other soft, light-colored wood will work as well.

CHOOSING A SURFACE

Many surfaces, or mediums, can be used for burning portraits. I love working on basswood because it is so soft and white, and the grain is so subtle, all of which combines to allow for great contrast in shading. I used basswood for all of the projects in this book. It's easy to find at craft supply stores and comes in a variety of sizes and finishes (square, round, with bark edges, etc.). Note that you'll need several 4" (10.2cm)-square by ¼" (6mm)-thick pieces of wood for the practice projects, a piece of scrap to use as a scratchboard (see page 33), and a larger piece of wood for your first project.

You aren't limited to basswood. Any soft and light-colored wood will work well. I also use linden, birch, maple, and Italian poplar plywood. I recently tried pear and it was wonderful. I dislike pine, however, because it is too knotty. Look for wood with grain that complements the portrait, and avoid wood with large blemishes that might end up in the middle of a forehead or cheek.

There are many other choices, as well. You can burn on heavy paper, such as watercolor paper. Vegetable-tanned leather is very smooth and easy to burn. Unbleached canvas and other natural fabrics will work, too. You could even burn a three-dimensional portrait on a gourd or artist conk (tree fungus).

As with any pyrography project, avoid manmade materials, such as plastic or acrylic, treated lumber, MDF, manufactured cork, glossy paper, or standard chromium-treated leather. These may give off poisonous fumes when burned.

WOOD GRAIN

Wood grain refers to the stratification of wood fibers in a piece of wood. Generally you'll want to use wood with mild grain and no knots for woodburning. Save your best clear pieces for portrait work! That said, however, one of the pleasures of working with wood is being surprised by the way the grain adds visual interest to the art.

No matter how clear the wood looks, invariably a stripe of graining will burn darker than the rest of the wood. When it happens, concentrate on sliding the pen smoothly across the surface rather than focusing on the amount of sepia value at that given moment.

You may also find that a particular heat setting burns lighter or darker than you expect in an area of the portrait. Most likely, this is due to an area of grain. Again, use a consistent "Smooth Shading" motion and glide past the problem. As you continue, you will burn past the harder section of grain and return to the softer wood, where the "normal" heat value will return.

Grain areas can show up anywhere on a portrait, and you need to be able to ignore them—keep your hand and smooth shading stroke even. (For more on Smooth Shading, see page 27.) You can return to the area later to burn more layers and blend it in or leave it alone because it now adds a great artistic look to the piece.

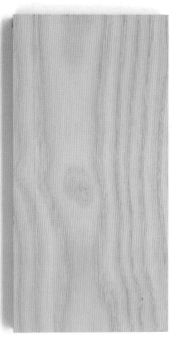

Wood grain refers to the pattern and texture, visible as stripes and whirls.

Prepare the wood by sanding it smooth.

WOOD PREP

I always pre-sand my wood until it is completely smooth. You can use a sanding block, a random orbital sander, or a drum sander—whatever you have. Start with coarser grain sandpaper, like 80 grit, and sand through the grits to 220. Rule of thumb: The surface should be "baby bottom smooth" before you begin burning. I do not use any type of sealer at this point.

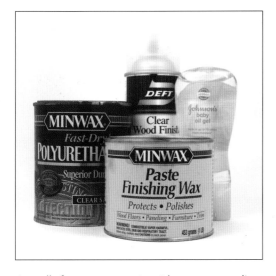

I usually frame my portraits with museum-quality glass. Other artists protect their work with spray or brush-on polyurethane. Experiment on samples and decide what you prefer.

PROTECTING YOUR PORTRAITS

There are a number of ways to protect a completed portrait. You want the burned texture to show through and not be covered up, but you also want to protect the surface from scratches and sunlight.

I usually frame my portraits with museum-quality glass. In addition to protecting the surface, it helps prevent fading from sunlight. If you prefer to display a piece without glass but know it will be near a sunny window, consider using a finish with UV protection, such as marine varnish. Pyrography can fade if exposed to direct sunlight.

I don't use varnish or lacquer—I don't like the way they change the color of the wood—but I sometimes rub baby oil gel into the wood with my fingers. I let it soak in for a couple of days and then wipe or buff with a lint-free cloth or paper towel. The baby oil gel, which contains mineral oil, really makes the darkest areas of the wood look deeper and richer. If you prefer, you can try tung or Danish oil instead, using the same procedure. They will add different colors and accents to the work.

Other artists protect their work with spray or brush-on polyurethane. Apply several light layers to build up the finish gradually, letting each layer dry thoroughly before adding the next.

Experiment with different finishes on sample pieces. Be sure you like the effect of the finish—both the color and the level of gloss—before you apply them to a completed portrait.

General Techniques

There are a few general techniques that you will use repeatedly in burning portraits. I'll describe them in detail here. Spend some time practicing each so you are familiar with them when you start the tutorials in Chapter 4.

Angle 1

Angle 2

Angle 3

Angle 4

ANGLES

I typically hold my pen at four angles while burning. Because the angle of the nib plays a large part in how I burn, I've made an illustration for you to reference. Use all of the angles with a very light touch so as not to leave depressions. The wood is going to shy away from high heat, but keeping a soft pressure will help smooth the surface.

Angle 1: Completely upright (90°). Because the metal of the nib is thin, it will slice into the wood. I use it for outside borders or other areas where a slice is not a problem or is desired. You can produce very fine hair if you use Angle 1 with the lightest touch possible over an already-burnished area.

Angle 2: Slight angle (60°). I use Angle 2 as I begin the delicate edges of skin. Using a lower heat setting, you can set the pen down at Angle 2 to make a nice clean edge, and then roll into Angles 3 and 4 as you slide and lift the pen off to the right.

Angle 3: More of a tilt (30°). There isn't that much difference between Angles 2 and 3; they just fit neatly between upright and flat!

Angle 4: Flat. I use Angle 4 for smoothing and blending.

As you can see, there isn't a great deal of difference in the angles due to the small size and shape of the burning nib. However, those small differences matter when it comes to the temperature you're burning and how much shading or value is needed. At Angles 1 and 2, there is not a lot of metal on the wood. As you lean, it directs more heat onto and into the wood. That is also why it's important to use the lower heat settings so you don't burn faster than you want to in delicate areas.

This view shows the area of the nib that should be in contact with the wood.

Smooth Shading Soundtrack

Music can help you burn! I look for instrumental songs in 3:4 time, which is great for making short strokes—1, 2, 3; 1, 2, 3; 1, 2, 3! You may laugh, but when faced with a few inches of very fine hair, the time will go faster when you get into a rhythm. I always select something soft, soothing, and tranquil with no words (although "My Favorite Things" from *The Sound of Music* does the trick, too!).

FLOAT OVER THE WOOD

Using a very light touch is critical in getting a smooth look. I will constantly repeat, *"Lightly* touch the wood," or, "Touch down and *lightly* slide…" Hopefully that will become ingrained by the time we get to noses!

Because I work in layers, many of the beginning stages look *terrible*! Try not to be discouraged. Once we add the layering and detailing, you will be thrilled with the outcome.

THE SMOOTH SHADING TECHNIQUE

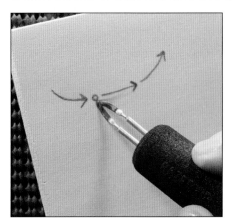

Start the smooth shading stroke by touching down gently.

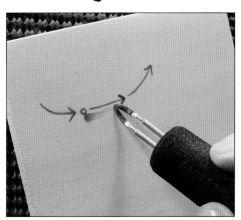

Slide to the right (for righties; reverse if you are left-handed) and then lift the nib.

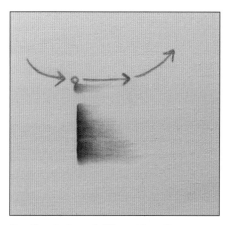

Practice strokes of different lengths.

Essentially, I use one stroke to do all of my burning. Whether I'm doing long burnishing strokes over a big, flat background or tiny shading strokes inside a nostril, I use a version of the same movement. I call it "smooth shading," and it consists of touching the nib to the wood, sliding, and lifting. You'll find increasingly challenging applications of this touch down–slide–lift stroke throughout the book. By the time you reach the mouth tutorial, having made this motion over and over, you will be on your way to being a top-notch portrait pyrographer!

You'll use different stroke lengths depending on what you're burning. I consider a medium-length stroke to be ¼" (6mm) or less. For most hand sizes, this will be a comfortable range to touch down–slide–lift. The longer

the stroke, the lighter the final area will be, because the nib cools as it burns.

Practice the stroke. Practice short strokes and long strokes. Practice gliding in smoothly as you touch down, sliding the nib evenly across the wood, and lifting off gently. (I am right-handed, so I slide from left to right. Lefties will do the opposite.) If the nib burns blobs, you need to touch down more smoothly. If the stroke completely fades away before you lift, you need to shorten its length. Pair smooth shading with the next technique, Turn the Wood, Not Your Hand, to make a sample board and really embed the motion in your muscle memory. (See page 21 for Sample Board instructions.)

Hold the pen in one hand and turn the wood with the other hand.

TURN THE WOOD, NOT YOUR HAND

When I burn, I hold the pen in one hand and use the other to move the wood. My burning hand and wrist are mostly stationary, while the other is almost constantly turning the wood to position it under the pen. This helps keep my hand, and thus the pen and nib, at the proper angle so I can repeat the touch down–glide–lift stroke over and over to create a truly smooth shading effect on the wood.

Practice burning a circle to teach your non-dominant hand to turn the wood so the dominant hand can continue making the smooth shading stroke. I typically burn clockwise around, but you should be able to burn just as well in the other direction, too.

BURNISHING

To burnish is "to make shiny or lustrous; to rub (a material) with a tool for compacting or smoothing." In burning, it means using the smooth shading technique paired with the lowest heat setting possible to smooth and flatten the wood fibers, thus making the next layer easier to burn.

Burnishing is critical in establishing a base color for the skin areas of a portrait. This base color should be as light as you can get it! Speed up the stroke to burnish the wood without adding color; if it's moving faster, the pen nib doesn't have time to reheat. You will darken skin by adding layers of heat on top of the burnished wood.

As you move from feature to feature, burnish all of the skin areas and the entire piece, sooner or later. This will assist in getting a very smooth transition and the ability to gradually darken or shade the skin. Set the heat to very low—we are not looking for "color," but to lay down the wood fibers. If you go slow and get a super-smooth base, you will be able to burn a little faster and with less fear of blobs later. Complete this step no matter what darkness the flesh will be at the end.

Not only does burnishing allow you to add color slowly, but it also shows which areas of the grain are more sensitive to heat. This will alert you to any problem grain lines running through the wood. (See Wood Grain, page 24.)

Burnishing is a rather boring part of burning, so I prefer to do it in bits and pieces rather than doing the entire piece at once.

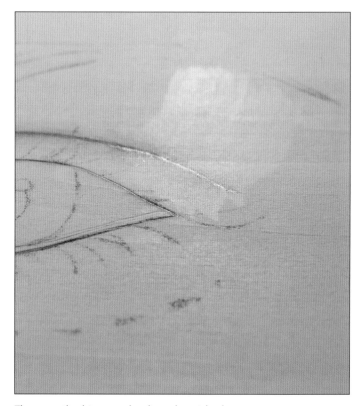

The smooth, shiny area has been burnished.

Just Three Things

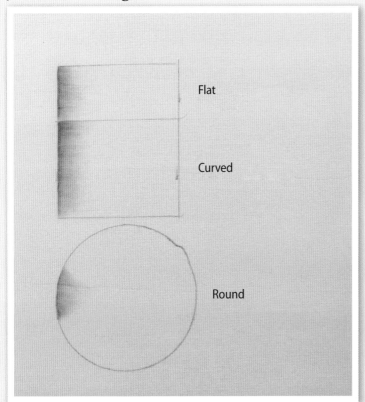

Flat

Curved

Round

We have established that with the smooth shading technique, you are basically doing the same motion over and over again, although sometimes with very short strokes and sometimes with longer strokes. The way you control the motion and the strokes creates flat, curved, or round shapes. And since most of the time you will be burning something flat, curved, or round, that means you only have three things to master!

Flat sections are created by filling an area with a solid burn.

Curves and round shapes are created by using a longer stroke and lifting at the end. The dark burns at the edges paired with the lighter center create the illusion of depth. This is how you begin the side of a face or the round areas of an ear. Highlights on skin and hair, and shaping of a cheek are all produced by this stroke. It's the same stroke used to burn inside a nostril, just on a small scale!

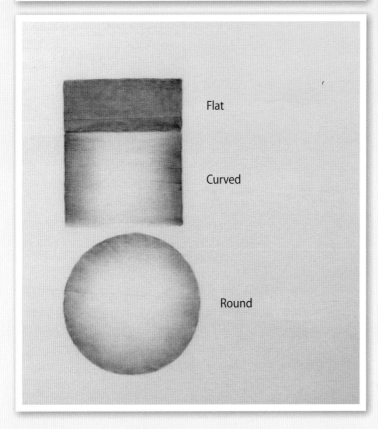

Flat

Curved

Round

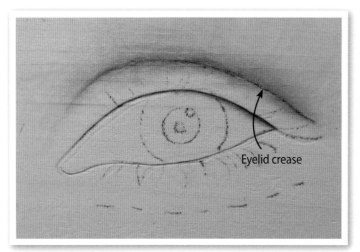

BURNING AN EYELID CREASE

An eyelid crease is a small thing, but the technique for burning one is fundamental to making many other features, including wrinkles and closed lips.

Eyelid crease

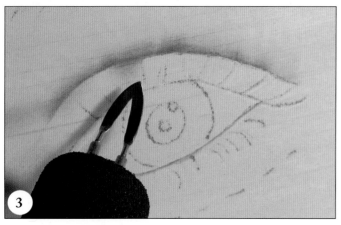

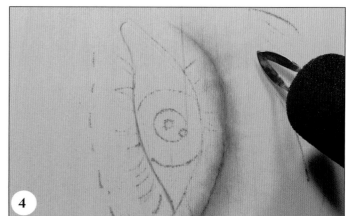

Step 1: Begin the crease in the center. The inside corner of the lid crease is lighter in value, so beginning in the middle of the crease gives you have more control. Touch down on the crease line and pull the shading toward the eyebrow, lifting the nib off the wood at the end of the stroke.

Step 2: Finish the line. Follow the crease line, remembering to lighten the area near the nose. The crease line should disappear into a smudge. Then work from the outside toward the center. Lightly erase some of the graphite.

Step 3: Burn the other side of the crease line. Turn the wood and work from the center toward the nose again. There isn't much distance here, so the stroke will be much shorter. Then work toward the outside.

Step 4: Extend the shading. Return to the section of skin between the crease and eyebrow. Touch down at the crease and pull the shading toward the eyebrow, lengthening the stroke and also burnishing the wood as you go.

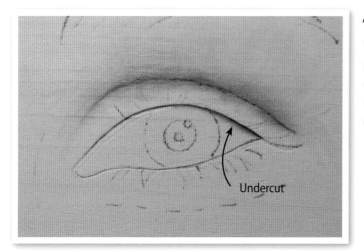

Undercut

THE UNDERCUT

Undercutting is a technique that uses shading to make an area appear to leave an overhanging portion or 3-D effect. This is achieved by layering the burn, *not* by actually cutting into the wood surface. I'll demonstrate on the eyelid crease sample.

Step 1: Outline the undercut area. We're going to undercut the top edge of the eye. Depending on the light source, there will always be an undercut somewhere on the eyes. Use Angle 1 and burn along the upper lash line to shape the eye. (Normally we would undercut after burning the lashes, but I did it before so you could see the technique clearly.)

Step 2: Until you are comfortable with this technique, turn down the heat a little so you can burn slowly. Use Angle 2 and trace the lash line a second time. Repeat the line one more time, using Angle 3. Notice that I confined the third shading line to the outside half of the eye line.

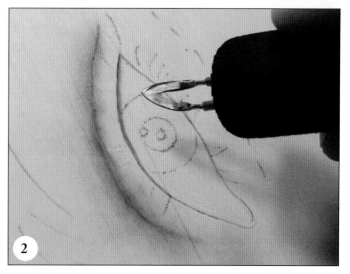

Definitions

Here are a few useful words, concepts, hints, and troubleshooting ideas that you might run across in the rest of the book.

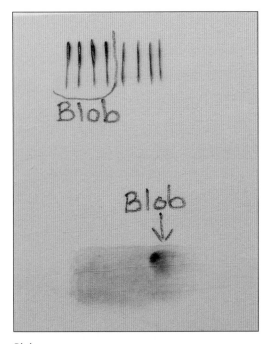

Blob

Burning Sleeve

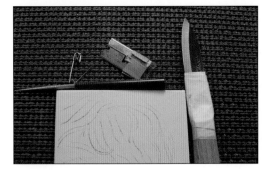

Cutting Tools

Blob: A small, dark area that appears within a perfectly smooth shaded section. A blob can happen on initial touch down or if the nib gets stuck in a section of grain. (Also known as a "Dang blob," depending on how often it shows up.) Alleviate blobs by "knocking off the heat" before resuming work after a pause. Blobs are also caused by high heat settings; turn down the heat and test it on a scrap block. You can sometimes disguise a blob by layering and blending the burn around it. You can also try very carefully removing it with sandpaper, but note that sanding undoes the burnish.

Burning sleeve: A material placed on your dominant hand to keep the oils and dirt on your skin from rubbing into the wood surface. Mittens or old socks work best.

Cut: Just as it sounds. Razor blade, tip of knife, safety pin, or other sharp instrument used to create light-colored (white, gray, or blonde) hair, whiskers, arm hair, etc. Keep a variety of sharp instruments nearby so you can choose one depending on how thick or thin the light hair is.

"Ffft" technique: A very subtle blending of a dark area into a light area. I use this sound effect, paired with a visual movement that is very hard to do in writing, when making short blending strokes. Previous students wondered how I was going to spell it. See the Nose tutorial on page 56 for an example.

Float: Gently touch the surface to glide over any rough areas without causing a blob.

Knock off the heat: A technique to reduce the heat in the nib after a break from burning. The heat builds up if you let the pen sit unused for a few minutes, so simply touch the tip to a scratchboard (scrap wood) before resuming the portrait, especially in very light areas.

Layer: A technique for building color in a pyrography. Using a lower heat setting, repeatedly burn the same area, going slowly, letting the darkness deepen gradually.

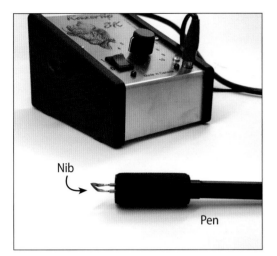

Nib and Pen

Scratch board

Nib: A fancy word for the tip of a burning pen. I'm using "nib" to distinguish it from helpful "tips," like listening to waltzes while you smooth shade. Some woodburning units have interchangeable nibs, while others have nibs permanently attached to the pen. My favorite nib is Razortip's Medium Spear Shader.

Pen: In this case, not a tube full of ink, but rather the handheld portion of a woodburning unit.

Pull shading: To color so that shades pass gradually from one to another, or to change by gradual transition. I use the term to determine the direction. "Pull the shading down from the hairline..." or "Pull the shading toward the center...."

Scratchboard: A scrap piece of wood kept nearby so that you can touch the tip of the burning tool onto it before resuming the portrait. (Save them—I've had people offer a good price for my scratchboards!)

Shadow lines: Lines in a pattern that represent gently burnished shadows rather than solid burned edges. I trace them with dotted lines rather than solid ones.

Smudge: A technique for adding a darker value by holding the pen tip flat so there are no actual lines or edges. Can be very light, such as the corner of the mouth, or larger and darker to create the arch of an eyebrow. Always touch down on a scratchboard before creating a smudge so you don't make a blob by mistake!

Value: The relative lightness or darkness of a color, or the relation of one part in a picture to another with respect to lightness and darkness.

Warm wood: Before you begin burning, the wood fibers are cold. The pen tip heats the subsurface, which in turn makes it much easier to coax a smooth burn. I like to envision it as in invisible cloud that you can push around as you continue to burn. You can see when the wood begins to accept the heat and change color; that's when things will start moving nicely. Be careful, though—the wood retains the heat and can burn you if you rest on it too long!

Safety

Never forget that the word *pyrography* loosely means "fire writing." You're working with a hot tool on a flammable surface, so you need to take a few precautions to keep yourself safe. At the same time, you're touching what you hope will be a beautiful work of art, so you need to protect the wood, too.

PROTECT THE WOOD SURFACE AND YOUR HAND

Your skin is covered in natural oils, sweat, dirt, and perhaps a layer of lotion. As your hands rest on the wood, all of that muck will transfer onto or into the surface you're about to burn, which will cause problems later. I always wear a covering over my dominant hand to keep the sweat and dirt off of the wood.

I like to wear a fingerless mitten, simply because I do not like having material between my fingers, as with gloves. You can cut the toe out of a sock to get started, or wear a leather glove (cut the fingers to suit) if you need more heat protection. I am also a knitter, so I make "burning sleeves" to match my socks!

I also use adhesive bandages on any fingertips that are getting too hot from long hours of burning. Just wrap them around any spots that are feeling too warm.

PROTECT YOUR LUNGS

Woodburning causes surprisingly little smoke, but you still don't want to breathe it. Work in a well-ventilated room, and use a fan to draw the smoke away from yourself (point it away from, not toward, you and your work). Finally, try not to hunch over your work. Sitting back a little will keep you from breathing the smoke and protect your back.

PROTECT YOUR HOME

Use some common sense to prevent harm to yourself and your surroundings.

- Always turn the burner off when you're not working with it.
- Always rest the hot tip in a holder or on a protective surface like a metal jar lid.
- Always turn off the machine to change pens or nibs.
- Never leave children unattended around a pyrography machine.

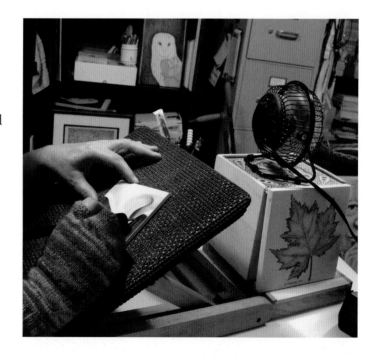

Chapter 3
Turning a Photograph into a Pattern

Luna by Juan Carlos Gonzalez of Madrid, Spain, is 5¼" by 18" and burned in poplar plywood.

On the one hand, you can turn almost any photo into a woodburned image. On the other hand, you're going to be spending quite a bit of time on this project; it makes sense to start with a nice photo so you end up with a great portrait. I will never be a great photographer, but by following a few simple rules and doing a little bit of digital tweaking, I can create an image that I can use for patterns and value guides to make a new portrait.

I liked this photo of a girl playing the violin, but the background was cluttered and distracting. When I burned it, I left in one wagon wheel for context but ignored everything else.

Choosing a Photograph

RULES OF COMPOSITION

It's probably no surprise that the same rules of composition that help a photo look great will help a woodburned portrait look great. If you are taking photos or looking through a selection trying to choose one for a portrait, keep these ideas in mind. If you have a photo you love that breaks all of the rules—go for it! Rules are made to be broken, and what matters is that you're starting with an image you like.

- **Fill the frame.** If you're doing a portrait, you want to see the person. Get closer, zoom in, or crop in and make that person fill the frame. This will also usually solve any background issues (see below).
- **Don't visually amputate the subject.** Judiciously cropping a photo is one thing; cutting off someone's ears is entirely different! Accidentally cropping out a guitar player's hands, for example, will change the whole impact of the image.
- **Simplify the image (aka, watch the background).** Sometimes a great expression or meaningful moment can get lost against a busy background. If you're taking the picture, either get closer to the subject or zoom in. If you're working with someone else's photo, use photo editing software to zoom in and get rid of the clutter. Unless context really matters, focus on the person, not the background.
- **Understand the rule of thirds.** Imagine lines dividing the image or scene into equal thirds, both horizontally and vertically. Then, place the main elements of the photo where the lines cross. This naturally sets up a pleasing, well-balanced image.

ABOUT INTERNET PHOTOS & CELEBRITY PORTRAITS

Photos on the Internet aren't free. Someone took them, which means someone owns them. If you see a photo online that you'd like to burn, ask permission from the photographer before using their work. I've made new friends by requesting permission. Imagine what they must think when you write: "Hey, I like your duck, may I burn it?"

In the case of celebrity photos, not only does the photographer own the particular image, but the celebrity owns the right to his or her own self image. So, technically, if you want to do a portrait of Johnny Depp, you have to get permission from the photographer *and* permission from Johnny. And if he's dressed like Captain Jack Sparrow, you have to check with Disney, too. The chances of someone suing you for copyright or trademark infringement are small, but why risk it?

Editing the Photograph

If you have a good photo to start with—one that's nicely framed and doesn't have a lot of background clutter—you might be able to skip the editing phase. If, however, there are elements you don't like in the photo, then a little photo wizardry might be in order.

PHOTO-EDITING SOFTWARE

There are any number of photo-editing programs, such as Photoshop and Lightbox, as well as a growing number of apps for phones and tablets. Some of them are even free! I use Corel PaintShop Pro (www.paintshoppro.com), which offers a free trial and then requires a purchase. Gimp (www.gimp.org) is very similar to Photoshop and free to download and use. Play with a few free trials until you find something you're comfortable with! Try following the pattern-making instructions below with the trial; that might be a good way to judge the software.

WHAT TO EDIT

My two goals when editing the photo are to crop and/or resize the photo and to remove distractions. In the case of distracting backgrounds, sometimes the cropping does the trick alone. Other times, as in the photo of the girl with the violin, you can simply ignore the background elements you don't like. I also use the editing software to remove or cover over things I don't want to burn into a portrait. For instance, in this family portrait, I did not want the green logo behind the baby's face, so I painted it out. I also think the mom's white arm distracts from the baby's silhouette, so I will burn that dark like the rest of her shirt. Look for little things like that to correct before you begin. Once you're happy with the image, print a color version to refer to as you burn.

Making the Pattern & Value Guides

I know a few artists who make their patterns by covering the photo with tracing paper and drawing guidelines by hand, and even a few who don't use a pattern at all. I use my photo editing software to first turn the photo into a black and white image that will be easy to trace and then to make a sepia-tone version that will serve as a guide to the tonal values in the burned portrait.

Making a Pattern: Corel PaintShop Pro

Pattern-making Notes

I will provide instructions to make patterns using a few common photo-editing programs. You should be able to apply the general ideas, if not the exact steps, to other photo-editing software.

Always work from a *copy* of the original photograph. If you save the edits to the original photo file, it will be replaced and no longer exist—you don't want that! Also, because every photo is different, you will need to tweak the basic settings until the resulting image is appropriate for the particular photograph you're working from. The beauty of these programs is that you can try something and simply hit the Undo button to make it go away. You can "undo" all the way back to the original if needed! You can also scrap the whole thing and start again, saving a new version from the original.

Step 1: Open and copy the photo. Click the Edit menu and select *Copy*. Return to the Edit menu and select *Paste As New Image*. Return to the Edit menu again and select *Paste As New Layer*. On the right side of the screen, you can see two small photos of my working photo: a background layer and a Raster 1 layer. (A "raster" is another name for a digital image made of pixels.)

 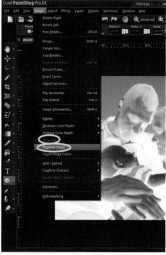 

Step 2: Make the photo black and white. Click the Image menu and select *Greyscale*. Return to the Image menu and select Negative Image. To the far right you now see that the Raster 1 layer changed with the selections.

Step 3: Blur the details. Click the Adjust menu and select *Blur* and then *Gaussian Blur*; set the rating around 23. Now it looks like you completely messed up the entire thing! Everything should be completely blurred out.

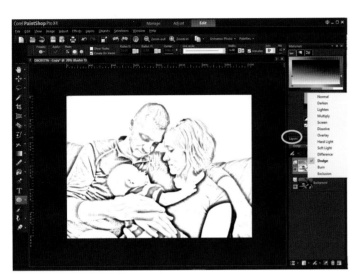

Step 4: Establish the basic pattern. At the far right, click the word Layers and select *Dodge*. That strips out the excess details in the image and creates the basic black and white pattern.

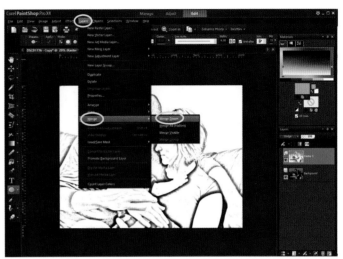

Step 5: Merge the layers. At the top menu, click Layers and select *Merge* and then *Merge Down*. When the step is complete, there should be one photo in the menu at right again. The two images--the original background and the outlined layer--merged into one.

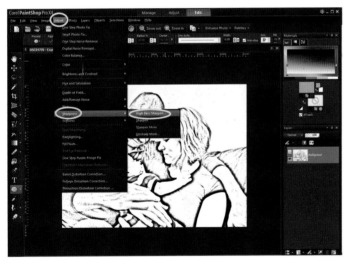

Step 6: Adjust the pattern lines. Click the Adjust menu and select *Sharpness* and then *High Pass Sharpen*. Another box will open with setting choices. Change the settings as follows: *Radius: 36; Strength: 100;* and *Blend Mode: Hard Light*. Your goal is to darken and clarify the lines to make the pattern easier to trace. Play around with these numbers to find what works best with the photograph you are using. If the pattern still doesn't have fairly sharp lines that seem easy to trace, Click the Adjust menu and select *Brightness and Contrast*, and then play around in those options until you get an outlined version of the image.

Step 7: Save and print the pattern. Save the pattern and then print it. This is the final that I ended up with after adjusting the *Brightness and Contrast*. Removing the color helps me see clothing folds, locks of hair, highlights, and shadows that I might overlook on the original color photograph. This will make tracing it onto wood easier.

Making a Pattern: GIMP

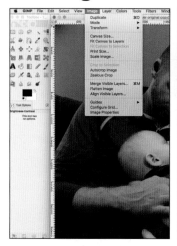 

Step 1: Open and copy the photo. Open the photo in Gimp. Click the Image menu and select *Duplicate*. A second image should appear. Close the original image. Click the Layer menu and select *Duplicate Layer*. In the pop-up Layers window, you should see two small photos of the working photo.

Step 2: Make the photo black and white. Click the Image menu and select *Mode* and then *Grayscale*. Click the Colors menu and select *Invert*.

Step 3: Blur the details. Click the Filters menu and select *Blur* and then *Gaussian Blur*; set the rating around 23. This removes details by completely blurring them out.

Step 4: Establish the basic pattern. At the far right, click the word Layers and select *Dodge*. That strips out the excess details in the image and creates the basic black and white pattern.

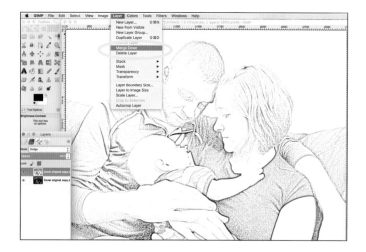

Step 5: Merge the layers. At the top menu, click Layer and select *Merge Down*. When the step is complete, there should be one photo in the popup Layers window. The two images—the original background and the outlined layer—merged into one.

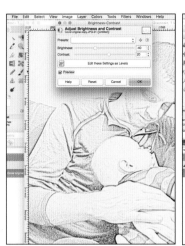
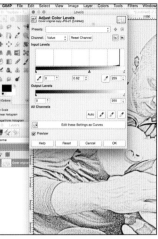

Step 6: Adjust the pattern lines. Click the Filters menu and select *Enhance* and then *Sharpen*. Another box will open; slide the bar to change the Sharpness setting (I started at 10). Your goal is to darken and clarify the lines to make the pattern easier to trace, and it may take some experimentation to find the setting that works best with the photograph you are using. Next, click the Color menu and select *Brightness and Contrast*. I set the Brightness to -40 and the Contrast to 20. You can also click *Edit These Settings As Levels* and play with the slider until you get an outlined version of the image.

Step 7: Save and print the pattern. Click File and select *Save* or *Save As*, name the pattern, and then print it. This is my final pattern that I ended up with after adjusting the *Brightness and Contrast*. Removing the color helps me see clothing folds, locks of hair, highlights, and shadows that I might overlook on the original color photograph. This will make tracing it onto wood easier.

Making a Pattern: Photoshop Elements

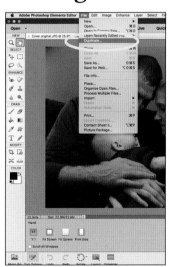

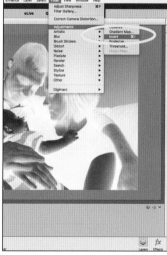

Step 1: Open and copy the photo. Open the photo in Photoshop Elements. Click on Expert in the top bar. Click the File menu and select *Duplicate*. A second image should appear. Close the original image. Click the Layer menu and select *Duplicate Layer*. In the pop-up Layers window, you should see two small photos of the working photo.

Step 2: Make the photo black and white. Click the Image menu and select *Mode* and then *Grayscale*. It will ask if you want to flatten the image before the mode change. Click *Don't Flatten*. It will ask if you want to discard the color information. Click *OK*. Click the Filters menu, select *Adjustments*, and select *Invert*.

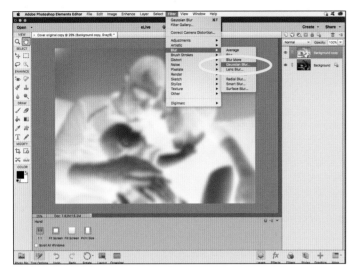

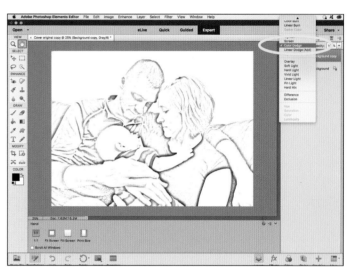

Step 3: Blur the details. Click the Filters menu and select *Blur* and then *Gaussian Blur*; set the rating around 23. This removes details by completely blurring them out.

Step 4: Establish the basic pattern. In the popup Layers window, click the word Normal to bring up a drop-down menu and select *Color Dodge*. That strips out the excess details in the image and creates the basic black and white pattern.

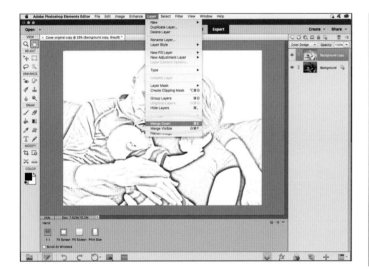

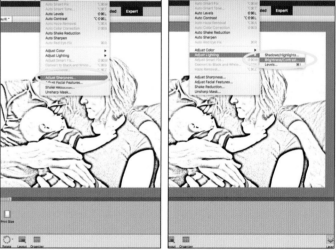

Step 5: Merge the layers. At the top menu, click Layer and select *Merge Down*. When the step is complete, there should be one photo in the pop-up Layers window. The two images—the original background and the outlined layer—merged into one.

Step 6: Adjust the pattern lines. Click the Enhance menu and select *Adjust Sharpness*. Another box will open with setting choices. Change the settings as follows: *Radius: 36; Strength: 100*. Your goal is to darken and clarify the lines to make the pattern easier to trace, and it may take some experimentation to find the setting that works best with the photograph you are using. Next, click the Enhance menu and select *Adjust Lighting*, and select *Brightness/Contrast*. I set the Brightness to -40 and the Contrast to 20, but you can play around with the settings until you are satisfied with the pattern.

Step 7: Save and print the pattern. Click File and select *Save* or *Save As*, name the pattern, and then print it. This is my final pattern that I ended up with after adjusting the *Brightness and Contrast*. Removing the color helps me see clothing folds, locks of hair, highlights, and shadows that I might overlook on the original color photograph. This will make tracing it onto wood easier.

Making a Pattern: Apps

On the one hand, there are tons of photo apps for your phone and/or tablet. On the other hand, most of them are intended to touch up selfies or create cool vacation photos. I played with a number of apps and found some that make the process easy—but it wasn't the apps I expected.

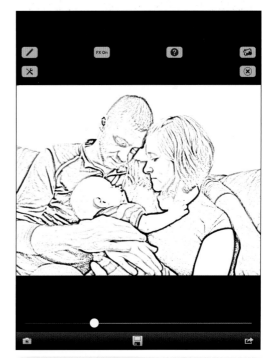

My first thought was to find tablet versions of the programs I used to make patterns—PaintShop Pro, Photoshop Elements, and GIMP—and see if the same instructions would work. Many good photo-editing apps are available, including PS Express from Adobe; Snapseed from Google; and Pixelmator. They are great for cropping, cleaning up backgrounds, and even making the sepia value guide. However, I couldn't recreate the combination of functions I use to turn a photo into a pattern.

Then I tried a different approach: sketch programs. These apps turn photos into sketches that look remarkably similar to our patterns! The apps allow different amounts of tinkering with the resulting sketch, so try a few to see what works for you. They are easy to find on the Internet and your device's app store; the two listed here are free. *Note: Remember to work on a copy of your photo.*

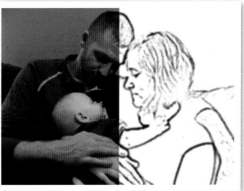

Sketch Me! (iOs, Android) and SketchFree (iOs): These free apps turn photos into sketches instantly. Just touch the photo icon and choose a photo; it will convert automatically. Most have sliders to adjust the details and line weights.

Making a Value Guide: Corel PaintShop Pro

I like to make a sepia-toned version of the photo to aid me in choosing color values while I'm burning. Sepia-toned photos, aka, "olde tyme" photos, are shades of brown, so they resemble woodburned portraits. It's like getting a preview of your woodburning with a few clicks.

Step 1: Open and copy the photo. Click the Edit menu and select *Copy*. Return to the Edit menu and select *Paste As New Image*.

Step 2: Make the photo sepia tone. Click on Effects and select *Photo Effects*. I choose *Sepia Toning* and set the number to 91.

Step 3: Adjust the tones. Click the Adjust menu and select *Sharpness* and then *High Pass Sharpen*. You may need to play around with the settings to find what you like best.

Step 4: Save and print the pattern. *Note: Print it in color.*

Making a Value Guide: GIMP

Step 1: Open and copy the photo. Open the photo in Gimp. Click the Image menu and select *Duplicate*. A second image should appear. Close the original image.

Take Notes!

As you experiment with your editing program, write down the steps you take as you do them. It will be hard to remember what you did. Plus, it can be helpful to read the help section that comes with your program!

Step 2: Make the photo black and white. Click the Colors menu and select *Desaturate*. From the pop-up menu, choose *Lightness* and *OK*. The photo should be black and white.

Step 3: Make the photo sepia tone. Go back to the Colors menu and click *Colorize*. You'll need to play with the settings; start with a Hue of 25, Saturation of 30, and Lightness of 5. If you like, sharpen the image by clicking the Filters menu and selecting *Enhance* and then *Sharpen*; slide the setting until you like the effect.

Step 4: Save and print the pattern. Note: Print it in color.

Making a Value Guide: Photoshop Elements

Step 1: Open and copy the photo. Open the photo in Photoshop Elements. Click the File menu and select *Duplicate*. A second image should appear. Close the original image.

Step 2: Make the photo black and white. Click the Filter menu and select *Gradient Map*. From the pop-up menu, click the little arrow next to the colors to bring up another pop-up menu. Select *Default* and click on the box for *Black, White*. The photo should look black and white.

Step 3: Make the photo sepia tone. Go back to the Adjustments menu and click *Photo Filter*. Leave the filter on *Warming Filter* and adjust the slider under *Density* to get the color you want. I used 80%. If you like, sharpen the image by clicking the Enhance menu and selecting *Adjust Sharpness*; slide the setting until you like the effect.

Step 4: Save and print the pattern. Note: Print it in color.

Making a Value Guide: Apps

Many phone and tablet camera apps come with built-in filters that will allow you to take a sepia-toned photo. So, if you are taking a photo specifically for a burning, switch filters and snap a few sepia-toned images, too. Working with an existing photo? No worries—many of the programs allow you to apply the filters after the fact. Here are a few that I've tried; experiment to find apps that work with your device.

Note: Remember to work on a copy of your photo.

Camera+ (iOs): Open the photo and hit Filters, Color, and Sepia. Click Advanced and play with the slider to adjust the color.

Sepia+Color (iPhone): Just open the photo and it's sepia. Play with the buttons and sliders to adjust the color. There are many similar apps for both iOs and Android devices.

Snapseed (iOs, Android): Google's photo-editing app is unusual in that you touch the photo, not a slider, to make adjustments. Open the photo and click the pencil icon. Choose Black and White and one of the selections; I used Bright. Click the checkmark. Touch the pencil icon again and choose Vintage. I chose option 2 and Blur Off. Then touch Adjust to bring up a menu with options such as Brightness, Saturation, and Style Strength. After touching a choice, drag your finger across the photo to see the effect; I liked a Brightness of -25, Saturation of 85, Style Strength of 85, and Vignette Strength of 30. When you're happy, touch the checkmark to save.

Instagram (iPhone, Android): Instagram's sepia filter works best on a black-and-white photo, so use your device's native camera app to change the photo first. Then, put your phone in airplane mode so the photo saves instead of posting. Open the app, choose the black-and-white photo, click Next, and choose the Earlybird filter. If you like, choose Edit and play with the options. Touch Share; it will fail and save the photo to your camera roll.

Transferring the Pattern to the Wood

There are a number of ways to transfer the pattern onto the wood. I use graphite paper and a pen to trace the details. This lets me choose which details to transfer; I try to do just enough to be helpful. I used to trace a lot of lines, but found that too many lines can be confusing when you begin burning. Graphite is also fairly easy to erase as necessary. For example, I don't want any lines left on very light areas of the skin or hair. *Note: Graphite paper and carbon paper are not the same thing; carbon paper does not erase.*

I do not use heat press or spirit transfer methods on portraits. Both of these methods transfer too many lines for my taste and can't be erased.

You'll need the black-and-white pattern, the wood, masking tape, graphite paper (available from art or craft stores; *not* carbon paper), a white artist's eraser (I use a Staedtler brand Hi-Polymer Eraser) and a red or blue fine ballpoint pen.

About Graphite Paper

I prefer used graphite paper to a brand-new sheet for portraits because we must be able to completely erase the traced lines. A fresh piece of graphite paper will copy too dark, so erase some or most of each line before you begin burning to get rid of the excess graphite.

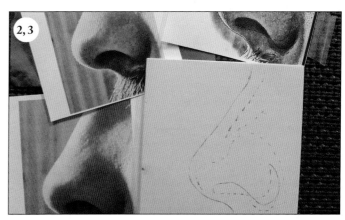

Step 1: Loosely tape the pattern to the wood, and then insert the graphite paper between the wood and pattern with the graphite (shiny) side down.

Step 2: Use a colored pen to trace the pattern onto the wood. Using a colored pen helps you see where you've traced. Check the tracing frequently to make sure lines are visible but not too dark. Use only enough pressure to draw the lines; try not to indent the wood. Be especially careful to press lightly when you are tracing the lighter areas of the face and skin. You want to be able to erase those lines easily.

Step 3: Use dotted lines to mark areas of shading or other "edges" that will not be burned as hard lines. (I call these

"shadow lines.") This helps you know how far to shade an area, but reminds you not to burn it as a hard edge. Mark the shadows just inside the actual area. This way you will burn over that line and have less chance of a traced line being visible.

Step 4 (optional): If you are working with a large portrait and pattern, you may wish to mark matching guidelines on the wood and pattern so you can re-tape the pattern onto the wood and retrace any details you may have missed or that were rubbed off by your arm.

Step 5: Finally, don't throw away the pattern. You will want to refer to it from time to time when you can't figure out some detail.

Chapter 4
WOODBURNING FACIAL FEATURES

Christian, 13" by 16", is by Dino Muradian of
Mississauga, Ont., and was burned on cardboard.

The following demo pieces will each fit on a 4" by 4" (10cm by 10cm) piece of wood. This is so that you can practice my technique on a quicker project size. I'll cover different angles or variations on some features so that you can refer back to this book when you are working on your own portrait and need a reminder.

We will begin as I do every portrait, with the eyes. Then we'll do the other features, and add the skin and hair. We'll take it slow, step by step and feature by feature. Once I get going on a portrait, however, I tend to jump around a lot. Don't worry—by the end of your first portrait, combining the features and working back and forth around the portrait will feel natural to you.

Eyes

I always begin portraits with the eyes. If you mess up the eyes, you ruin the whole piece and will need to start over! I may not always complete the eyes before moving on to other parts of the face, but they will be pretty close. Thanks to my daughter Kendra for the use of her "good eye."

We are starting our lessons with the eyes for another reason, too. The eyelid crease is the fundamental skill for working with faces, and we'll learn that here. You'll use the same techniques for making noses, wrinkles, lips, and more. Steps 2–3 explain the eyelid crease; you'll want to refer back to this section as you move on to the other tutorials in this chapter.

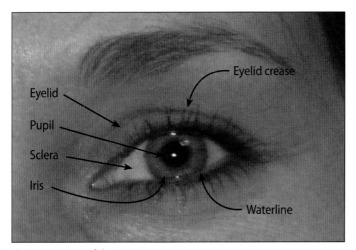

Common parts of the eye.

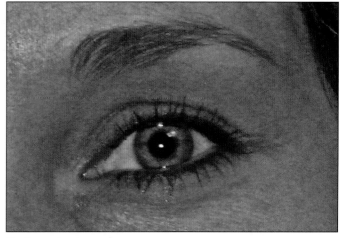

Sepia tonal-value pattern.

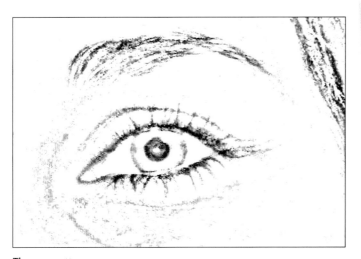

The eye pattern.

The finished eye.

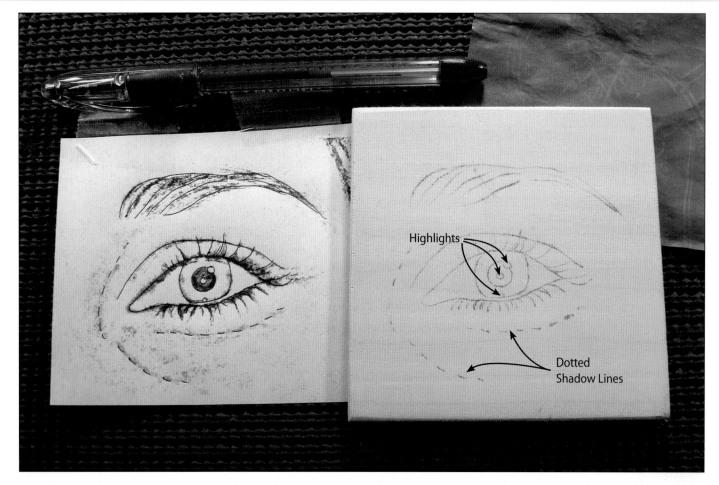

Getting Started

Refer to the instructions in Chapter 3 to transfer the pattern onto a practice board. As you trace the pattern, notice how I used a broken "shadow line" to show where there are changes under the puffy part of the eye and around the area that deepens right before going into the nose. There will be many areas that will not be burned as a line, but we mark them so we know where to begin or end the smooth shading. Also notice that the blue ink line from my pen stands out against the black lines from the printer so I know what I've traced.

Note, too, that there is a narrow "shelf" to the bottom eyelash section that is sometimes called the waterline. In the pattern you can see it from the middle of the eye to the outside corner. When I traced the outline of the upper and lower lashes, I followed the lash line but not the waterline. I don't trace the waterline because it is a very light area of the eye

Keep the Pattern Nearby

Keep the pattern nearby after you've finished tracing it, so you can refer to the lines drawn on it and compare them to what you are seeing on the wood.

where it can be difficult to erase the graphite. However, I will shade the waterline later.

Look at the highlights. Highlights make eyes sparkle! However, this particular eye has four white dots. If you have good control over the nib, you may choose to leave them all in, but if you are a beginner, just do two highlights.

It is important to notice these fine details, because they make the eye look real.

Finally, refer to your heat sample guide (see page 21) and choose a darkness equal to my #4. If you're nervous, lower it. Remember that for portraits, we like to err on the side of burning too light so we can return and burn again.

Eye: Burning the Eyelid Crease

1 **Outline the eye.** Begin at either corner. Turn the wood, not your hand, and follow the lines. The inside corner has that tiny racetrack turn, so keep the nib at Angle 1 and take baby steps to get around it.

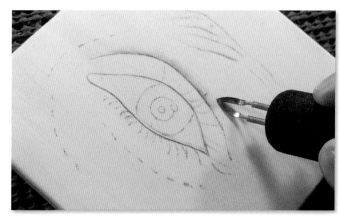

2 **Begin the eyelid crease.** Don't start at the very inside crease line. Give yourself room to return to blend it in once you have burnished the area. Touch down on the crease line and pull the shading up toward the eyebrow.

3 **Finish the eyelid crease.** Turn the work and shade the crease toward the lashes.

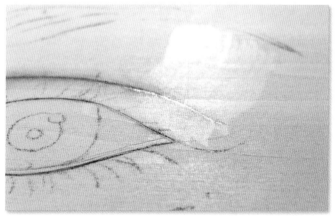

4 **Burnish the lid.** Use the same heat setting to burnish from the lid to the eyebrow; just use a faster slide. Lower the heat setting if your burnish doesn't look shiny, smooth, and colorless, like mine.

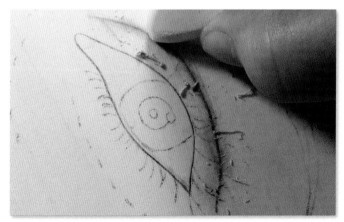

5 **Erase the crease line.** I typically choose to erase the crease line once I have worked it, being careful to leave the traced eyelashes. *Note: If your traced graphite lines are very dark, partially erase them before burning.*

Turn Your Photo Upside Down

The same way you turn the wood as you work, you should also turn the refernce photo. Placing the photo upside down helps you burn what you actually *see* and not what you *think* an eye (or any other feature) should look like.

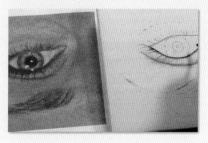

Eye: Burning the Lashes

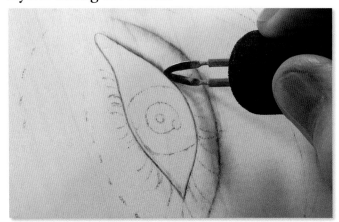

6 **Smooth shade the upper lash line.** Turn the work so you can touch down at lashes and use a short stroke to darken the lash line. You shouldn't need to increase the temperature.

7 **Begin burning the top lashes.** Use Angle 1 and a very light touch. Turn the wood frequently and touch lightly so as not to slice into the wood. Increase the temperature and work slowly to lay the burn across the surface of the wood.

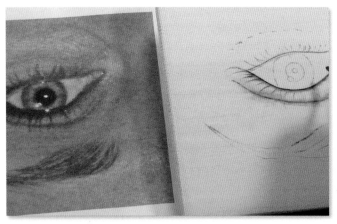

8 **Check your work.** Place the sepia photo and the project piece upside down so you can see where to place the upper eyelashes. Lashes are always varied—some can only be hinted at, while others are so long and curvy they cast a shadow. Placing the photo upside down helps you burn what you see and not what you think an eye should look like.

9 **Burn the lower lash line.** I start in the darker outside corner of the eye and work toward the inside. Reduce the heat if you turned it up for the upper eyelashes.

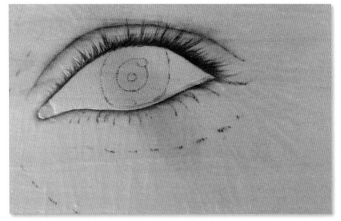

10 **Burnish from the lower lash area to the cheek area.** Burnish the tear duct in the inside corner as well. Then, increase the heat as needed and burn the lower lashes.

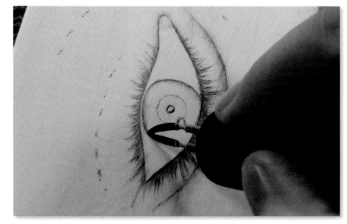

11 **Circle the highlights.** Then, use Angle 2 to shade the outer iris edge. Turn the wood as you go around the iris.

Eye: Burning the Pupil

We use the smooth shading stroke to burn the iris, but in micro movements. The slide and lift are almost one motion because the slide is so short. We do not want a solid iris, but we do want a solid pupil (except for the highlights).

If you choose, you can cut in or make a depression in the wood for the highlights before burning them to keep them light in color (the pen will glide past the depression). I typically don't need to do that unless the eye is very small. I prefer to cut a highlight before I burn, versus cutting into the wood later to restore a highlight that was accidentally burned over.

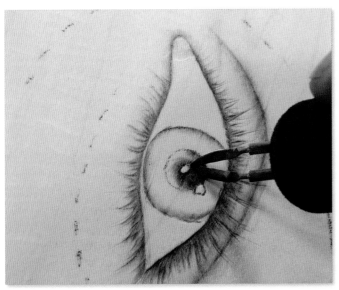

12 **Fill in the pupil.** Turn the temperature up a little, but use layering, not high heat, to get a dark value. Continue to turn the wood as you go around the pupil.

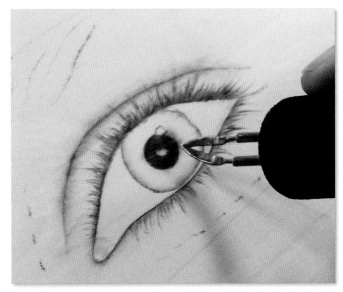

13 **Color the iris.** Turn down the heat and lightly pull color from inside the pupil to the iris. Every eye has different markings inside the iris area; try to match them.

14 **Burn the perimeter of the iris again.** Leave the heat reduced and burn around the outside of the iris again, pulling more shade toward the pupil. Do not fill the iris with solid color. Even if the subject has dark-brown eyes, use this type of shading to create different levels of sepia.

15 **Shade the waterline.** Burn over it very lightly. Also, burn very lightly over the inside corner tear duct glob. Begin rounding the sclera by touching down at the duct glob and shading toward the iris.

Eye: Forming the Eyebrows

Note: This is where I typically stop working on the eyes and go on to other parts of a portrait. I'll return later when I know how dark I want the eyes. If necessary, I will go over the crease, lashes, and pupil again to achieve the right tonal value. The more layers of color you do, the more realistic the eyes will be when you finish the portrait.

16 **Undercut the upper lashes.** This isn't really cutting. Slide the nib under the upper lashes to create a shadow line across the upper eye. Angle the nib so there is a wider shadow at the outside corner that tapers as you get to the inside corner. Increase the heat enough that you can glide over the wood, but still achieve a darker value. I undercut the eyelash three times.

17 **Shade the eyebrow.** If the person has light hair, lightly shade the brow shape and then erase the lines. It is hard to erase lines for hair after you've burned them, so the graphite might show behind light eyebrows. Otherwise, increase the temperature and follow the natural growth of hair on that particular person. Depending upon the thickness of hair, you will want to use a combination of Angles 2 and 3.

18 **Burnish the eye area as needed.** If you burnished from the lashes to the brow, toward the nose, and down toward the cheek area in Step 10, you are ready! Otherwise, burnish those areas now. Work slowly and enjoy the process.

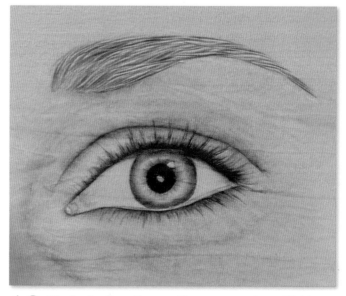

19 **Shade the dotted areas.** Do not trace them. Hold the nib at Angles 3 and 4, and repeatedly burnish and lightly shade the under-eye area. Erase any remaining graphite lines, and set the piece in a location where you can admire your work!

EYE VARIATIONS
Asian Eyes

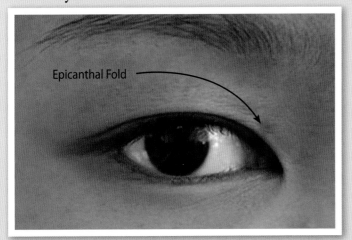

Epicanthal Fold

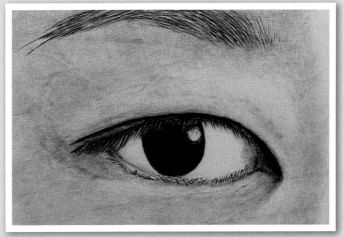

The epicanthic fold gives Asian eyes their unique appearance. Burning an epicanthic fold is similar to making an eyelid crease: first pull the shading up toward the eyebrow, and then pull it toward the eyelashes. Notice the direction these eyelashes grow.

Dark Eyes

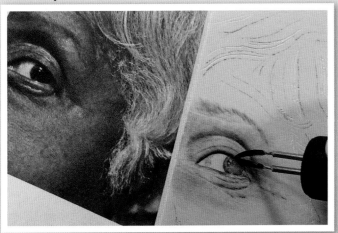

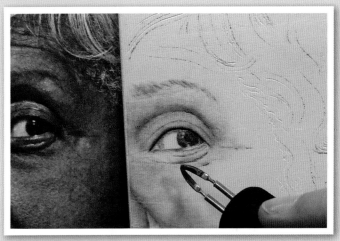

This eye has a very dark iris and no lashes to speak of, and is surrounded by darker skin tones. I follow my usual method for eyes but increase the heat a little to assist in creating the darker tones. To burn the puffy lines under the eye, use the method for the eyelid crease, but with smaller motions, and smooth over them with a burnish.

Elderly Eyes

The eyes themselves don't change with age, but the skin and features around them do. In this example, the eyelashes are thin and growing in several directions. The eyelid crease is sags and bags, so I only use the smooth shading stroke from under the brow line to just before the eyelashes. I cut in three white eyebrow hairs before I began burning. They blended in as I burnished the skin, but add to the appearance of age and make the brow bone more prominent. The wrinkles are just like tiny eyelid creases. Follow the line of the wrinkle using very short smooth shading strokes. Then, turn the wood, do the same short smooth shading stroke the other way, and finish with a smooth burnish. Finally, increase the heat so you can barely touch the nib of the pen to the wood surface and redraw the tiny wrinkles.

Nose

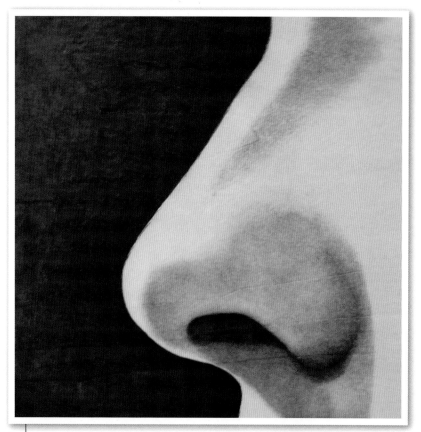

A completed nose.

Noses come in so many shapes and sizes that it was hard to pick one (pun intended) to use as an example. I opted to ask my son-in-law, Joe, to pose for this one. Luckily his nose is pretty small, so this can be a quick project!

When you combine a nose with lighting, there will always be a shadow somewhere on the face. It could be under the nose, extending to the upper lip, or on the cheek beside the nose, as in the example photograph. We will shade the side of the nose for contouring and then burn over the contour shading to make shadows! Sounds simple, right?

You will recognize some of the eyelid techniques in our work on the nose, and this will, in turn, serve as preparation for working on the ear in the next section.

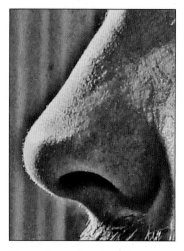

The sepia version of the nose photo; use this as a value guide.

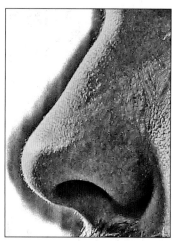

The nose pattern.

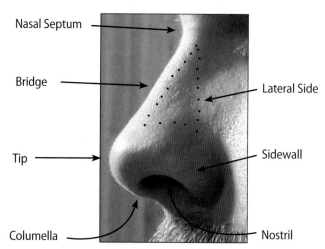

Nasal Septum

Bridge

Tip

Columella

Lateral Side

Sidewall

Nostril

The nose has a few basic parts that we can easily identify whether we are looking at it straight on or from the side.

Nose: Outline the Nose

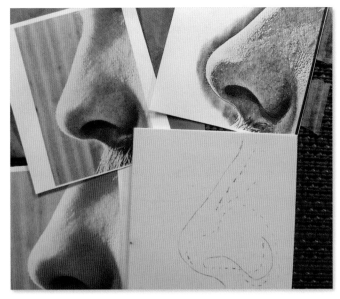

1 **Trace the pattern.** Use solid lines to outline the shape and dotted lines to make the shadow areas. Pay attention to the nostril area. When you burn, you will want to know where to stop with the darkest value and begin the contour shading.

2 **Create the highlighted edge.** With heat set at about 5.5 and the work turned upside down (for right handed artists), use the smooth shading stroke to touch down at the outside edge of the nose and slide to the right. I touch down with Angle 2 at the edge and then flatten to Angle 3.5 by the end of the stroke/lift. (Don't flatten the nib completely; you need to keep the edge a bit higher than the wood surface to clear any new grain lines and get a smooth liftoff.)

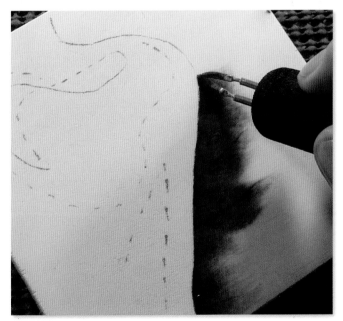

3 **Burn around the nose.** Turn the wood as you go around the tip of the nose. Don't press harder or turn the burner up to create darker lines. Instead, layer the strokes to warm up the wood subsurface and extend the length of each stroke. I work 1" to 2" (25mm to 51mm) at a time, layering, smoothing, and pulling the shading to the right.

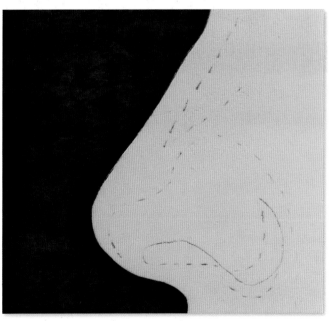

4 **Darken the background.** Erase the outside edge lines once you finish.

Nose: Contour the Nose

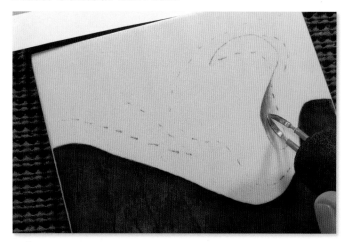

5 **Reduce the heat to setting #4.** The darkest edge of the nostril is at the top. Turn the wood so that you touch down at Angle 2 in that top area and slide toward the dotted line. Repeat two or three times.

6 **Dealing with grain lines.** Notice that on my sample, a grain line is not changing color. I ignore it for now and continue with the smooth shading strokes. I will return to the nostril later and blend that streak in as necessary.

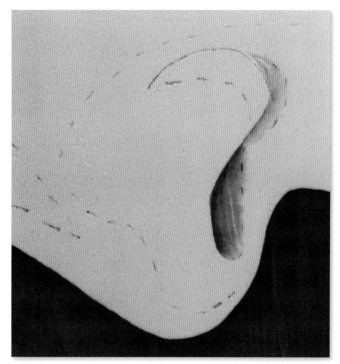

7 **Shade the under side of the nostril.** Reduce the heat to setting #3. Turn the wood and begin to shade the under side of the nostril, blending the lightly shaded area into the darker space. I touch down inside the dark cavity and lift right before the edge to leave a strip of white where the edge of the skin glows from the light source.

8 **Shade over the sidewall.** Turn wood and shade from the bottom of the nostril over the rounded sidewall area to the dotted line. Stop before reaching the dotted lines. You can blend this area later.

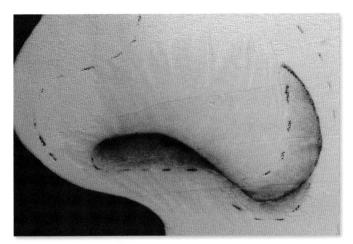

9 **Burnish around the nostril.** Reduce the heat to setting #2, or the setting that creates a little color when layered two or three times. Burnish around the nostril. Then, begin contouring by touching down inside the darkest space and round over the skin/sidewall of the nose to round the nostril.

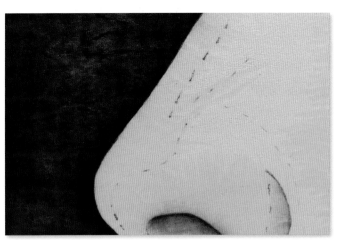

10 **Burnish the bridge of the nose.** Reduce the heat to setting #1 to burn the lightest value. Using Angle 2 or 3, touch down in the dark portion of the background along the bridge of the nose. Burnish with a longer stroke into the dotted lines that mark the shading on the side of the nose. Burnish below the nose (the mustache location) and the right side of the square where the light shines on the cheek.

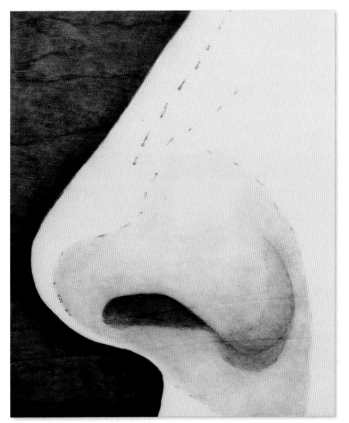

11 **Add more layers.** Repeat the previous steps to add more layers of burning and make the skin a deeper, richer value. When you drew the dotted lines, you stopped a little short of the actual shadow line. Now as you add layers to those dotted areas, extend the shading over the dots and then erase them.

12 **Burn the shadow beside the nose.** Begin in the middle of the dotted V shape using Angle 4 and heat setting #3. Remember to knock off the heat so you don't create a blob where you set down.

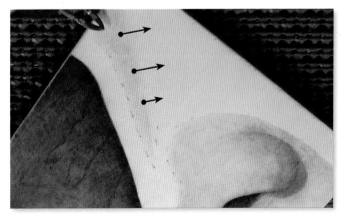

13 **Complete the shadow beside the nose.** Turn the wood, begin again in the middle, and slide to the side.

Nose: Complete the Nose

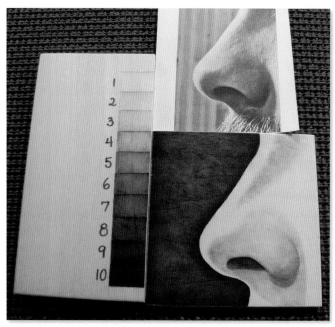

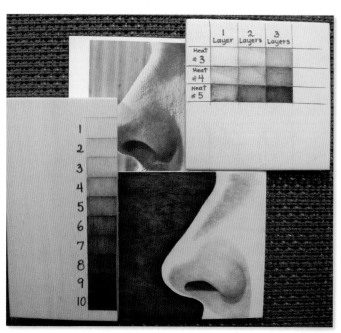

14 **Compare the work to the value guide.** Set the value guide next to the work and the copy of the sepia photo. Where do you need to increase the values on the nose? Read the next step before you burn.

15 **Compare the work to the layer guide.** Set the layer guide next to the work. Check the heat setting and layers you need to achieve the goal value and start burning again. I am having you work very slowly at contouring the nose so you can practice the smooth shading stroke. As you become familiar with shading, you can use a higher temperature to achieve results more quickly.

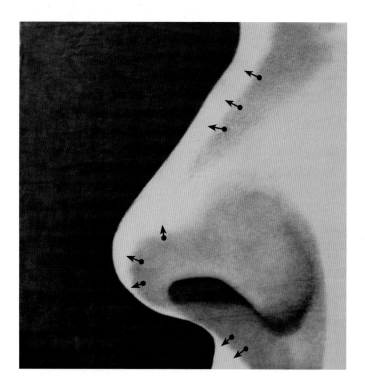

16 **Use the "Ffft" movement to blend the shading along its edges.** Look at the shading along the bridge of the nose. There is quite a contrast between the source light and the shading . With the heat at setting #2 or #3 and the piece upside down, touch down into the shaded area and quickly "Ffft" into the source light area. This very subtle blending really adds to the overall effect. One layer of "Ffft" usually completes the blend; I rarely do more than two layers of it.

NOSE VARIATIONS

Front-facing Nose

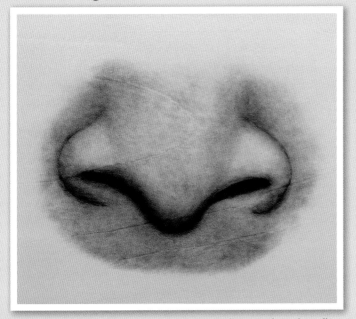

To create "lift" on a front-facing nose, touch down at the columella, or underside of the nose tip, and pull the shading up toward the bridge. Turn the work and touch down at the same location and pull down toward the lip.

Top-lit Nose

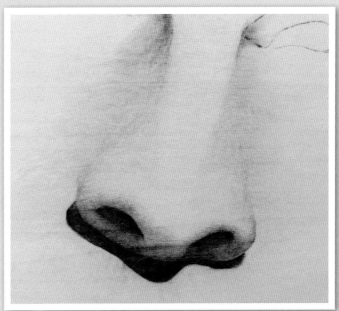

A strong light source from above leaves a very prominent shadow under the nose. Darken it appropriately to create the contour of the nose tip.

Nose with Mustache

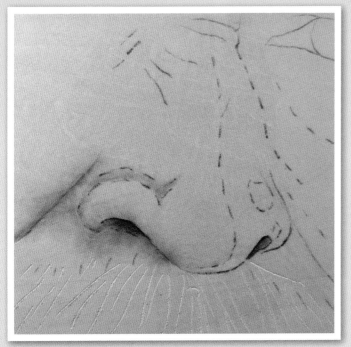

This nose hangs down over a mustache. I used dotted lines to guide where the shading stops. The cheek lines are burned just like an eyelid crease. First, touch down on the "line" and pull the shading toward the nose and mustache. Then, turn the wood to touch down on the "line" and pull the shading toward the ears.

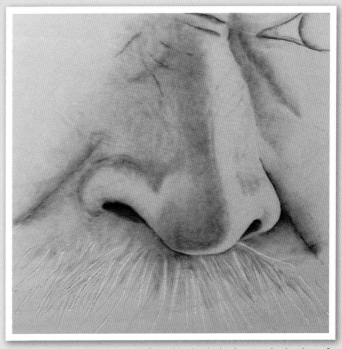

Use the "Ffft" technique to soften the shaded edge on the bridge of the nose. The one line of shading under the nose makes it appear to be sitting on top of the mustache.

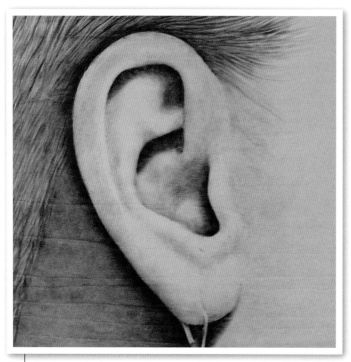

The finished ear.

Ears

Burning the ears builds on the techniques we learned while burning the nose. The nose was larger and allowed for a longer stroke. With this ear, you will have to shorten the smooth shading strokes to fit into the tighter spaces. Thanks to my daughter Kaysha for the use of her ear.

Some parts of the ear have dark shadows—the antihelix under the upper section of the helix; inside the concha area; and the ear canal. We will burn these just like we did the nostril: we'll touch down at the darkest edge and pull the shade toward the center, turning the wood continuously to keep the hand and pen tip in the correct position.

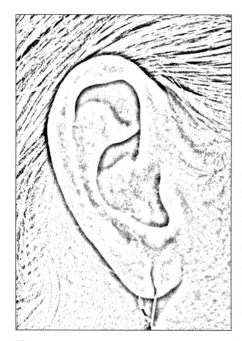

The ear pattern.

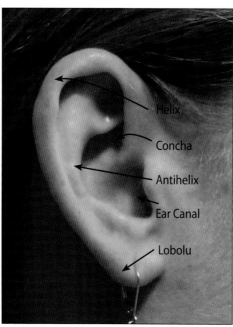

The parts of the ear.

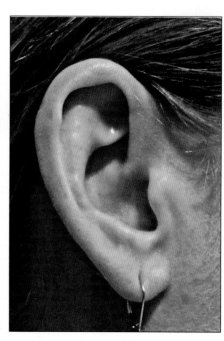

The ear sepia value guide.

Ear: Getting Started

1 **Trace the pattern.** Refer to the sepia value guide to see where the shading and shadows are. We highlighted the nose by burning a solid background. Ears are generally surrounded by hair, so I traced a few to give a little practice in working it. Plus, knowing where the little hairs are in front of the ear tells you where to place the subtle shading.

Ear: Shaping the Inner Ear

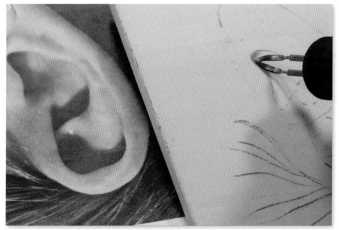

2 **Begin with the ear canal.** I am using the Medium Spear Shader, although I would switch to a Small Spear Shader if the ear were any smaller. Using heat setting #4, begin with the ear canal area and follow the dark area up toward the bottom of the helix. Constantly turn the wood. Small space, small turns.

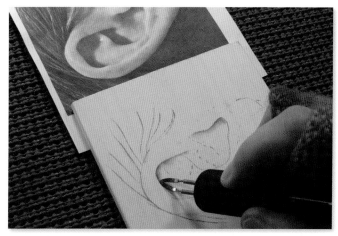

3 **Shape the inner ear.** As you round the ear and begin to descend along the inner edge of the helix, the sharp edge, or fold, of the ear flattens out to become the lower lobule. This is a lighter area of skin, so partially erase the traced line if it's dark so you don't burn a crease that doesn't actually exist.

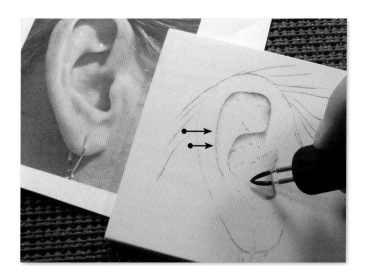

4 **Finish the inner ear.** With the work upright and using Angle 3, slide the nib from the area of darkness at the top, down along the curve about midway, and lift. We will finish the lobule area and merge into that blended line later. Burnish any light areas within your reach; we'll come back to add shading and depth in values. As you become more relaxed about burnishing, you will do it automatically.

Ear: Shaping the Lobe (with Earring)

Before starting on the outside edges of the ear, let's look at the earring. The wire is tiny and has little room for error. We will use the concept of burning behind an object to bring it forward. Because this is a very small area, use heat setting #4 or lower so you can leave the tip on the wood longer without scorching the surface. Burn in layers even in this small area so you can match the depth and value along the rest of the ear. If you prefer, erase the earring and treat the lobule as unadorned (but where's the fun in that?).

5 **Shade the loop.** I start with the right side, and then turn the wood to shade inside the loop.

6 **Accent the front part of the wire.** Use the smooth shading technique, but squish it into one very small touch-lift movement. With the heat lowered, you can pause at the touch down to let the value deepen. Do not try to fill the wire with shading. The tiny areas left white will make it look as though the silver is shiny.

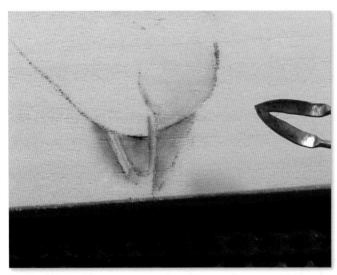

7 **Shape the back portion of the earring wire.** On my printed copy, I could make out a single line of darkness. Use Angle 1 and a very light touch to carefully place the line in the center of the wire. Notice I did not shade behind the back wire until I did that step. (Had I missed the center, I would've made the back section wider!)

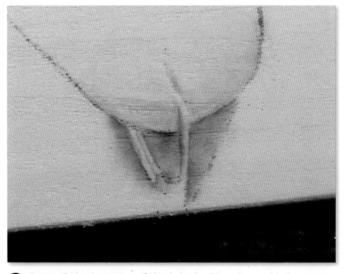

8 **Round the bottom of the lobule.** Use the smooth shading stroke and Angle 3 to blend a smudge of color where the earring pierces the skin. Don't poke or make a dot; I aimed for a hint of a depression.

Ear: Detailing the Outer Ear

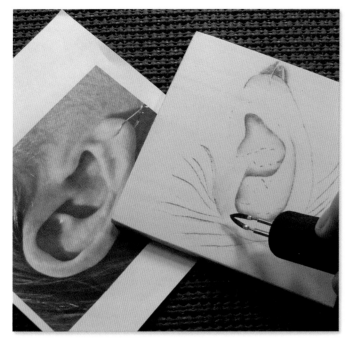

9 **Shape the outside edge of the ear.** I like to start at the top. That is where the highest concentration of light is, so it will be the whitest for highlighting. Use Angle 3 and smoothly round the shape, turning the wood as you go.

10 **Add some wisps of hair.** Increase the heat to setting #5 and use Angle 2. Trace a few of the pattern hairs as a guide to show how the hair flows around and behind the ear. Once you have burned a few of the guide hairs, erase the traced lines.

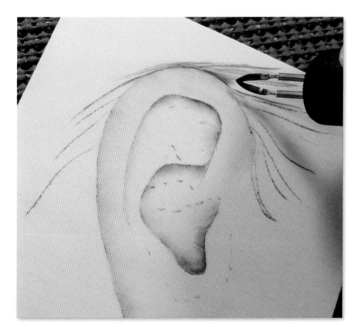

11 **Shade the top of the ear.** Touch down at the edge of the ear and pull the shading along the hair toward the temple. At the top center, don't worry about following the hair flow; instead, be careful to build the burn slowly at the skin edge to make the hair appear to be in back of the ear.

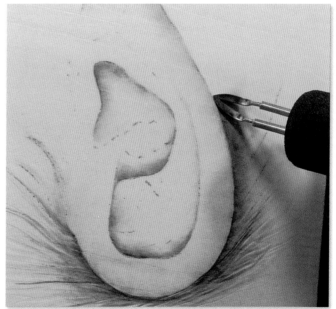

12 **Shade behind the ear.** Turn the wood and use the same technique behind the ear. Touch down at the edge of the skin and pull the shading out to the right. The hair doesn't hang down behind the ear, so the smooth shading turns into just shadows as you near the lobule.

Ear: Undercut the Ear

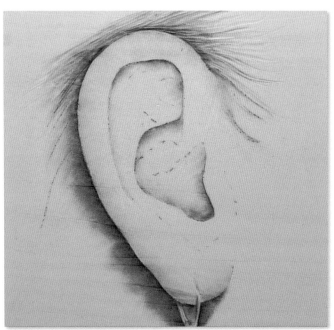

13 **Undercut the ear.** The technique will make the skin line appear to be raised. First, round the outside edge of the skin. Reduce the heat to setting #4. Touch down in the darkest area behind the ear and smooth shade over the skin at Angle 3. (You used this technique to round the nostril on the nose.) Notice that the upper portion of the ear is almost flat compared to the lobule. In that area, still touch down in the dark background and round over the skin edge, but move quickly to Angle 4 so you can shade it to look flatter.

14 **Shade and burnish the edge of the ear.** Turn the piece upside down for ease in creating the value. This is a slow process at heat setting #4. Pause at the edge to let the value begin to change, and then slide. Because the tip will cool quickly, this is a good time to burnish the rest of the ear near where you are working.

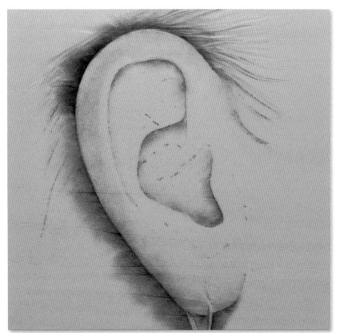

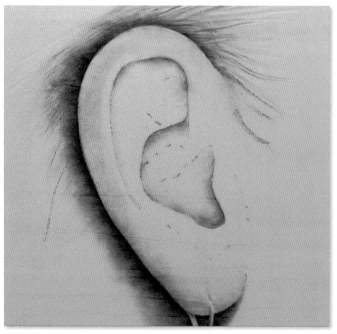

15 **Re-burn the dark background behind the ear.** Turn the heat to setting #5 and lightly touch at the junction of darkness and skin, pause, and slide to the right. The higher temperature will make the wood depress on its own; you do not need to apply pressure, and you do not actually cut. You want a smooth surface.

16 **Re-burn around and behind the earring loop.** Match the values with those behind the ear.

Ear: Adding Depth to the Ear

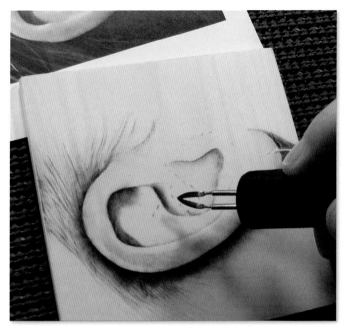

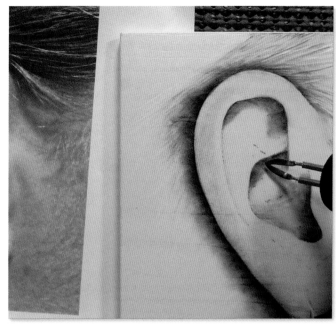

17 **Pull the shading across the concha dark area into the shadow of the helix.** Use Angle 3. There will still be shading down to the top area of the helix as it flattens into the ear canal, which will make the area appear to stand out from the inner ear. Also, finish burnishing inside the ear, in front of the ear, where the cheek and hairline meet, and under the ear where the earring hangs.

18 **Shade the darkest shadows.** Increase the heat to setting #4 or #5. Touch down in the dark area and pull the shading into the ear. Look at some areas that may only get one layer. Little folds and joins really don't need a dark line.

Ear: Finishing the Ear

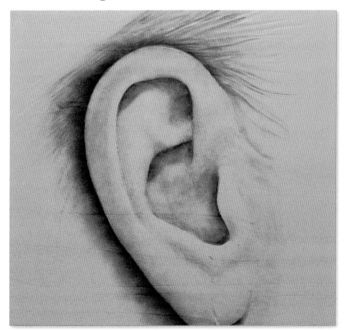

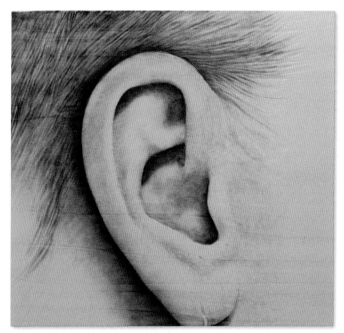

19 **Continue shading and shaping the interior of the ear.** Use a lower heat setting and Angles 3 and 4. Note that where the helix merges into the antihelix, there is no defining line. If the model were standing before you, you might see more of a separation. However, we are burning what we see and we do not see anything but light and shadows there.

20 **Add some hair (optional).** It will emphasize the edge of the skin and help give the illusion of the ear sitting on top of the wood. If you chose not to do hair, simply fill in with a solid background. Let the value lighten to nothing at the temple area.

EAR VARIATIONS

Front-facing Ear

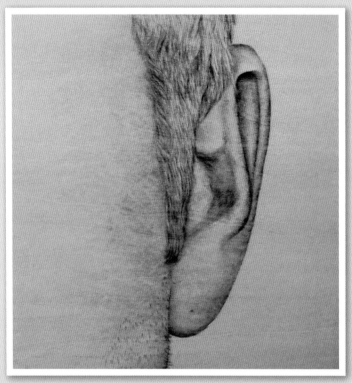

The more you stare at ears, the odder they look. Now that you have burned the sample ear, you should be able to identify its parts from different angles. To burn a front-facing ear, use the shading and roundover techniques; don't burn a line where there is none.

Mouth

One of the biggest mistakes is burning lines where there are none. On the ear, we had folds, dips, and grooves, but we didn't give all of them a hard edge; instead, we hinted at them by lightly shading over them. When we do the mouth, we will hint at the shape of the lips, hint at the teeth that are barely visible, and shade the philtrum. Notice how I used dotted shadow lines when tracing the pattern to hint at areas of shading, like under the chin and the cheek area beside the nose.

When cropping the sample photograph of my daughter Kelsey, I included the nose so you could match the values inside the nasal cavity with those inside the mouth. (Plus, it is a chance to practice that area again!)

I selected the previous sample projects to make it easy to show you how to use the smooth shading technique. For the mouth, we will use a profile that is not so easy. You are ready!

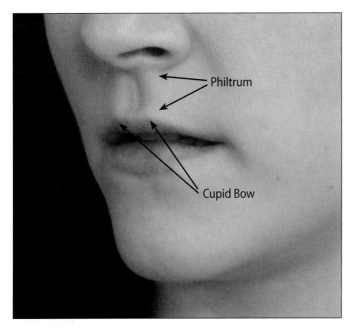

The areas of the mouth.

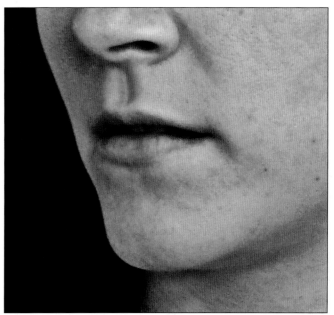

The sepia value guide.

The pattern.

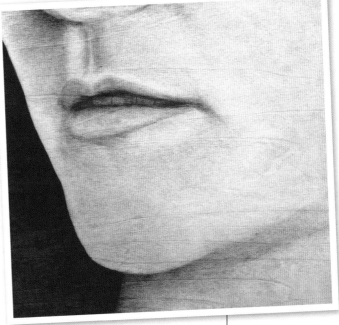

The finished mouth.

Mouth: Burn the Background

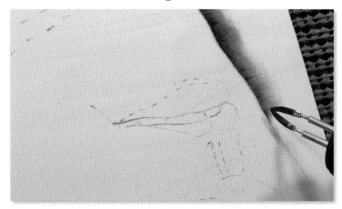

1 **Create the edge by burning along the cheek profile.** Use heat setting #5 and turn the wood as needed. You may need to increase the temperature if the pen is not getting the same result as the sample photograph. Aim for a deep color like value #9 or #10.

2 **Fill in the background.** Burn in layers and use Angles 3 and 4 as needed. Notice that a grain line does not burn at the same temperature as the surrounding area. I will return later to blend it in if needed. I burned three layers on the background before moving on to the next step.

Mouth: Establish the Lips

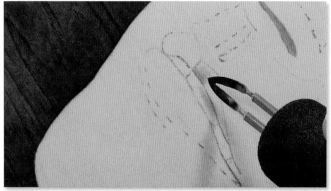

3 **Begin the upper lip.** Adjust the heat to setting #4. For an open mouth, begin burning the upper lip by touching down at the center opening and pulling the shading up toward the cupid's bow. Because of the profile view, the upper lip is curved, so watch how it drops down around the teeth at the left side of the photo. The model's lip is not full, so you end up with more of a shadow than a lip line in that corner.

4 **Burn the left side of the upper lip.** Begin at the top portion of the lip using a flatter Angle 3 so as not to make any lines. Pull the shading down into the open mouth. Once that area is shadowed, turn the work, touch down at the open mouth, and pull the shading up onto the lip.

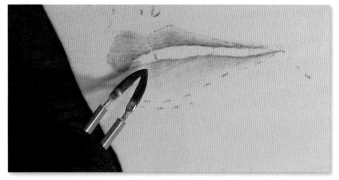

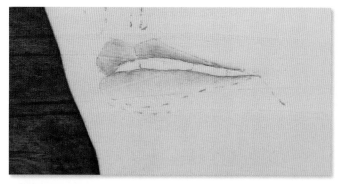

5 **Burn the lower lip.** Use the same technique: touch down in the center and pull the shading toward bottom edge of the lip.

6 **Redraw the teeth.** You should have what appear to be very white teeth between slightly parted lips. We will not detail inside the mouth right now, but it is a good time to study how far toward the center of the mouth the shadows reach. Use a graphite or soft lead pencil to redraw any missing teeth details. The teeth will be shaded, so darker traced lines are okay.

Mouth: Establish the Nose

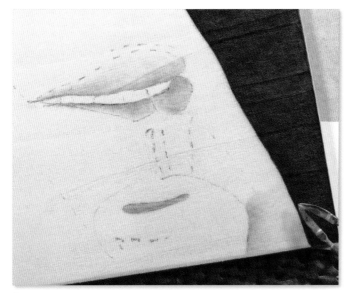

7 **Shade the cheek "behind" the nose.** Reduce the heat to setting #3 and shade behind the nose so the tip appears to sit higher than the cheek. Stop the shading at the traced lines; however, you can speed up the stroke to slip over the edge into the darkest background. Speeding up the stroke allows you to burnish the wood without adding color because the pen tip doesn't have time to reheat.

8 **Burn the nostril.** Now that you have already burned a nose, doing the smooth shading style around the nostril should go quicker.

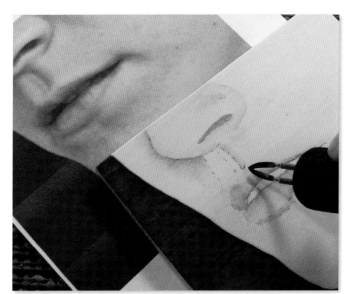

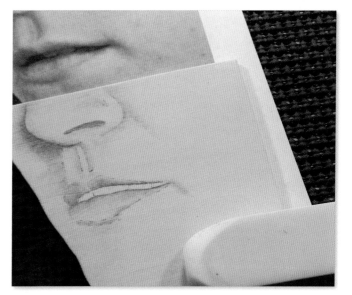

9 **Shade the philtrum area above the upper lip.** Remember that dotted shadow lines indicate you should not burn a hard edge; instead, gently shade using Angle 3. Burnish the rest of the face, referring to the tonal values and layer guides to create skin tone. Remember to knock off the heat from the pen tip any time you pause to prevent blobs.

10 **Smudge the mouth.** The corners of the mouth are shaped simply by smudging each area with a shadow. Begin with a light smudge in one corner of the mouth. As you burn the skin tones, return to the corner and re-darken the smudge to keep it a value or two darker than the skin. Take the time to erase as you develop the shaded areas.

Mouth: Define the Chin

11 **Define the chin.** Because the neck is under the chin, begin shading by touching down at the junction and pulling the shading down.

12 **Round the chin.** Turn the wood, touch down at the junction of the chin and neck, and pull the shading up toward the mouth. That smooth stroke instantly rounds out the chin.

13 **Shade the jawline.** First turn the wood so you can shade down the neck, and then turn again so you can slide up onto the jaw.

Mouth: Shade Inside the Mouth

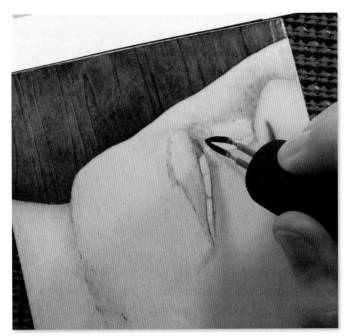

14 **Begin shading the left side.** Touch down at the inside upper lip and pull the shading toward the lower lip. Because this is a small area, I use Angle 2 for better control. Press lightly!

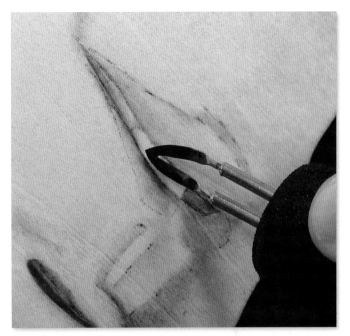

15 **Undercut the upper lip.** For the eye sample, we used an undercut on the top row of lashes to give a shadow effect to the eye. For the slightly open mouth, we will do the same thing along the upper lip to create a shadow along the teeth. Shade the upper teeth in two passes, first using Angle 2 and then using Angle 3 to widen the shadow.

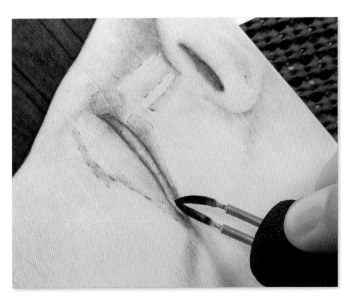

16 **Repeat the undercut.** Turn the wood and repeat the undercut from the bottom lip to blend into the shading on the teeth. I only did one pass.

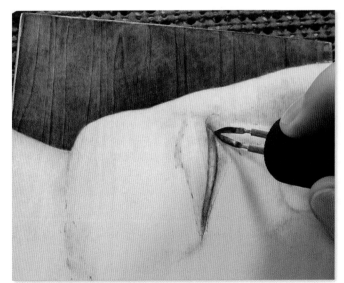

17 **Shade the teeth.** Touch down at each inside corner of the mouth and pull the shading toward the center teeth. Notice that both corners of the mouth are dark and the value lightens toward the center. The teeth should be completely shaded by now.

Mouth: Finishing Touches

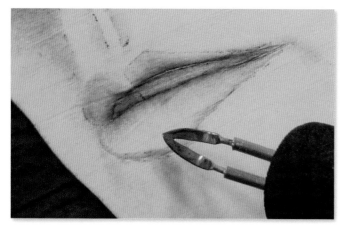

18 **Detail the mouth.** Return to the upper lip and smooth shade up. The final values should be a layer or two darker than the skin.

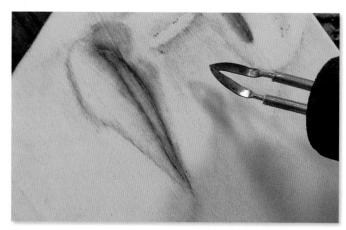

19 **Burnish the skin.** If you haven't already, lightly burnish the entire skin area of the sample square. Take the time to make it smooth, because you will need to slide the pen tip around at Angle 4 to burn the subtle value changes.

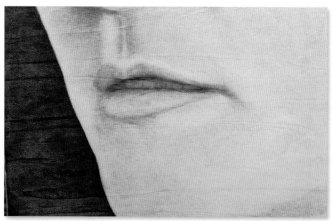

20 **Lower the heat to setting #4.** Hold the pen at Angle 4 to slowly build the skin values. Lightly float over the surface of the burnished wood, so you can easily control the change and blend the color. There is no crease line to the right of her nose, just shadow areas. The same is also true for the corners of her mouth and under the nose.

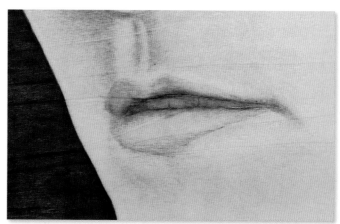

21 **Blend the edge of the face.** The source light gives a white or lighter edge to the face. Use the "Ffft" technique to blend from the dark to the lighter edge of the face.

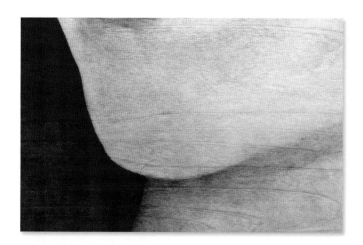

22 **Undercut the chin.** When you are satisfied with the skin values, undercut from the chin down to the neck so the rounded chin will look like it is raised from the wood. Done slowly and in layers it becomes a very smooth transition.

MOUTH VARIATIONS

Full Lips With Lipstick

For white teeth—everything around them must be darker! Using a higher temperature for the lips creates the look of lipstick. The heat setting is very low to shape each tooth. There is no hard "outlining" to them.

Baby's Mouth With Little Philtrum

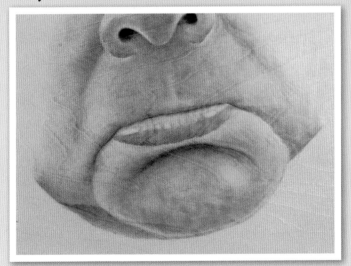

To create the depth under a baby's pouty lip, burn two steps, just like an eyelid crease. Notice the corners of the mouth are smudges. I left white (unburned) highlights on the lower lip to give the impression of dampness. Each nostril was burned from the inside top area and pulled out, even though it's a very short distance in a baby's nose.

Irregular Teeth

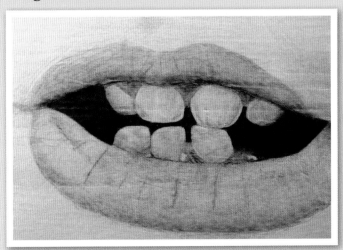

Not all teeth are picture perfect. I did not burn any harsh lines to make these teeth. I burned around them with the very dark background, and I used a lower heat setting to burn the gums. All that was left was to burn lightly all the shading variations on each tooth to match the original photo.

Hair

The model for this tutorial, Jackie, has beautiful white hair cut in various lengths. Her style includes a longer section at the crown, bangs, curls at the forehead, and short, wavy hairs in the sideburn area. In short, it's one head of hair that is perfect for practicing a number of hairstyles!

I burn the hair after I am fairly satisfied with the face, so you will see Jackie's completed eyes and skin in this tutorial. I have not included those instructions here, but you can refer to the earlier sections of the book and burnish and burn the skin, at the very least. It's good practice and helps you see how the skin relates to the hair. I usually start the ears before I do the hair, if they show, to help define their locations in relation to the hair, and then develop them along with the hair. (Be careful not to burn over any hair lines that overlap the ears.)

I suggest you do all of the steps for this tutorial, but when you're doing hair for a portrait later, you'll want to skip around and do just the parts that are relevant. If the ears don't show, for example, you don't need to shade behind them!

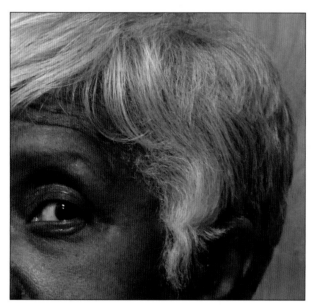

The original photo.

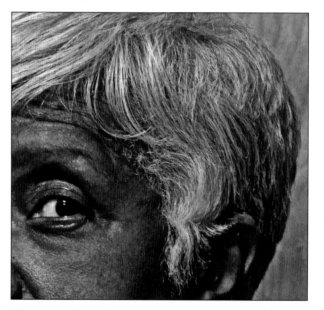

The sepia value guide.

The pattern.

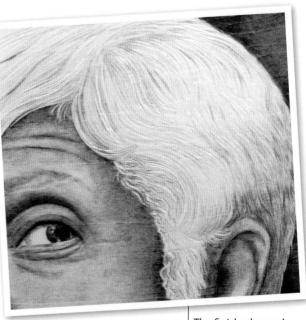

The finished sample.

Use Used Graphite Paper

When you burn light hair, whether it's blonde, white, gray, or red, don't use a new piece of graphite paper to trace the pattern. You will erase (or partially erase) many of the hair lines you trace, which is made more difficult by dark new graphite lines.

Cutting in Highlights

I discovered by trial and error a method for creating a lifelike effect for light-colored hair, whiskers, or eyebrows, whether they are blonde, white, gray, or even light red. After tracing the pattern but before you begin burning, literally cut lines into the wood to represent the very lightest hairs. The nib won't reach down into the cut, so you'll maintain a very light area even within the light burnishing.

To make the cuts, I keep a number of edged tools in my woodburning kit, including a paring knife, a razor blade, and a medium-sized safety pin, and I use whichever best fits the diameter of the light hair in the portrait. I like using the paring knife for long, straight or curling hairs. A pointed file rolls nicely for easier curly hair, but is harder to control through odd grain formations. For this tutorial, I used the pointed round file for the temple and sideburn areas, and the paring knife for the longer hair in the bangs and at the crown.

You do not have to cut every single hair; just do the very lightest or those you particularly want to highlight. Use light pressure as you cut to control the movement. You can always go over the hair a second time if not deep enough.

Some of the wood fibers will splinter and raise as you cut through the grain. I usually leave those alone until I am further along in the burn, to see if they will lay down again as I detail the rest of the hair. If not, I use the tip of a razor blade to carefully remove anything poking up. (I am not a fan of using sandpaper on surfaces that I have already burned.)

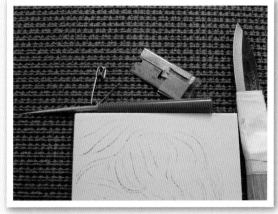

Cutting tools: a pointed file, safety pin, razor blade, and paring knife.

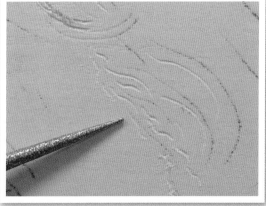

Literally cutting in the lightest highlights ensures they will be visible against the burnishing.

Hair: Defining the Edges of the Hair

1 **Define the edges (optional).** While dark hair will stand out against a light background, light hair needs a dark background for contrast. Adjust the burner to setting #5. I began burning "behind" the head at the base of the neck.

2 **Hair rarely has a smooth edge.** You'll need to leave the short flyaway hairs. Make the edge of the hair jagged. Turn the wood so you can burn from the outside edge of the piece toward the subject. As always, burn in layers, letting the background deepen slowly and smoothly.

Hair: Starting the Hair

In earlier tutorials, we burnished the wood to set the lightest value for the piece. Here, we cut the lightest hairs into the wood; everything else will be somewhat darker. With light hair, the differences in those values will be very subtle.

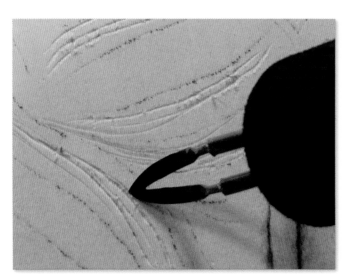

3 **"Sketch" the burn.** Use heat setting #3 or #4 and Angles 2 and 3. Following the direction the hair is combed, lightly burn a few guide hairs. Place the strokes beside (not on or over) the cut hairs and the graphite lines. The slower you pull the stroke from the crown to the bangs, the lower the temperature should be. Erase lines as you work so you don't accidentally burn them into the wood.

4 **Add more cuts as necessary.** If you think you don't have enough highlights, cut a few more with the tool you used earlier. Deepen the original cuts, if desired. Burn a few more guide hairs. (I know it looks bad. Hang in there—it will look better!) Change the pen angle to #3 and #4 to slide or glide over the "light hairs." Be careful as you burn the hairstyle near the longer cuts so you don't slip down into the grooves.

Hair: Flowing Hair Around Ears

5 **Begin shading and detailing around the upper ear.** Avoid burning into the light hairs that overlap the ear. Shade the hair behind the ear to bring out the ear.

6 **Burn a layer of hair over the head.** Burn individual hairs, following the traced and sketch-burned pattern lines. Think of these as layer one. You will add many layers to give the effect of thick hair.

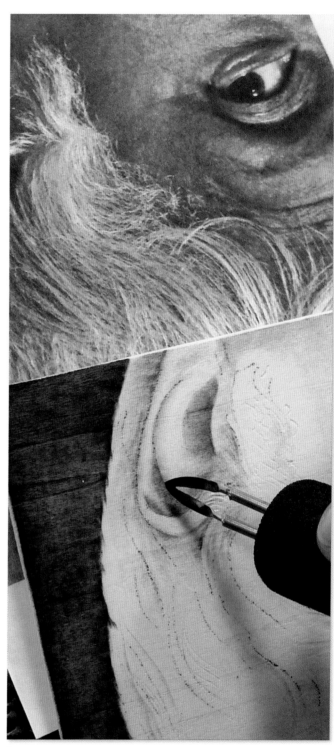

7 **Add more details in and around the ear.** Increase the temperature if needed. Burn the layers slowly so nothing gets darker than you want. Turn the wood as needed, and refer to the sepia value guide often.

Hair: Filling in the Sides

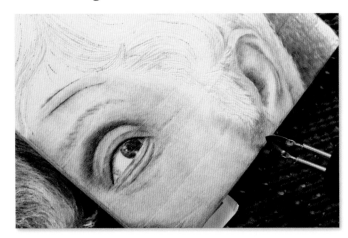

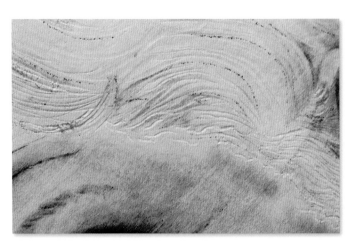

8 **Burnish the area between the hair and the ear.** Use Angle 1 and lightly touch down to create the individual hairs. Then, begin matching the skin values around the side hairs and detail the ear to match. I do a lot of jumping around at this stage. I burned a little at the side, then went to the ear to match values, then burned the hair behind the ear so it keeps up with the depth, too.

9 **Smudge the lightest hairs.** Hold the pen at Angle 4 to slide over and near the cut light hairs. I call it "smudging" because there are no real start or stop edges.

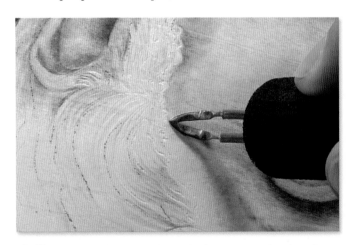

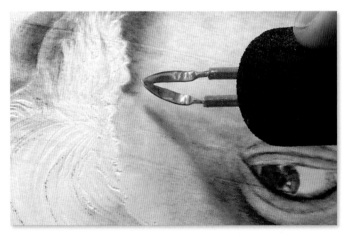

10 **Burnish the area where the hair meets the skin.** I use the V point of the nib and heat setting #4 as I burnish along the hairline.

11 **Detail the sides.** The temperature is still at setting #4, but let the nib rest or pause before pulling the shade toward the center of the face. Make the strokes small and very delicate, skimming over the surface. That will make the darkest values at the edge of the hair with a smooth transition to lighter on the cheeks at the end of the stroke.

12 **Blend the cheek area.** When the hair reaches a desired value, transition to Angle 4 flat and gently blend into the cheek area with a back and forth motion. Return to any other areas that need to match in value, such as the eye, ear, or hair behind the ear.

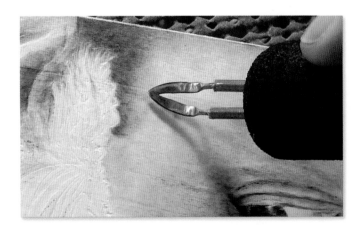

Hair: Burning the Hairline and Bangs

13 **Begin the forehead.** With the temperature at setting #4, place a light line beside the first light hair in the bangs. Go slowly to avoid the pen tip slipping into the groove. This will be the beginning of the undercut we do to make the hair appear to be raised from the skin.

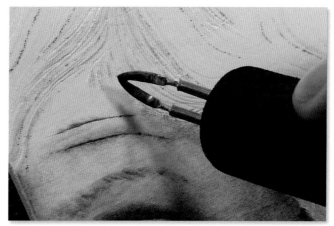

14 **Burnish around the wispy light hairs cut at the beginning.** Turn the wood to place a line along the rest of the hair, meeting up at the temple. You should have burnished most of the forehead when you did the skin. Now, work from the hairline and blend into the previously burnished skin. Rework the wrinkles, eyebrow, and anything that needs to stay darker in value than the skin.

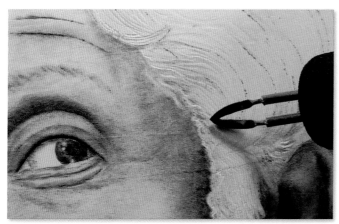

15 **Match the skin values.** Referring to the sepia value guide, look at the skin underneath the fine hairs along the temple and side area. Once you have the skin value to your liking, begin placing that same value in between the hairs. Use the tip of the Medium Spear Shader and slow strokes. Do not burn in the light cuts. Let the wood "cook" to the desired value.

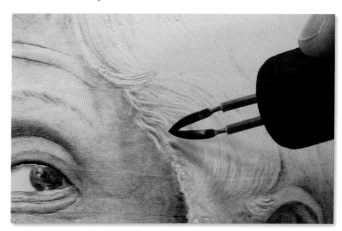

16 **Fill in more hair.** Refer to "Burning Strands of Hair." This is a sample so you can try out all the variations. You do have to follow the natural hair flow, but you can turn the work upside down, too.

Burning Strands of Hair

The pencil drawing shows the different designs I use to portray depth in the thicker areas of hair. Make these pen strokes by simply turning your wrist as you burn the single hair.

To create the look of a shadow along the length of a hair, I begin a hair stroke holding the pen at Angle 2, roll slightly into Angle 3 to thicken the line, and then return to Angle 2 to finish with a narrow line.

Sometimes I burn a shape that reminds me of a narrow wishbone with one leg longer than the other.

Similarly, you can burn two lines that begin together, part in the middle, and then rejoin at the end. As a variation, darken the open middle by rolling or changing the angle of the pen.

Hair: Final Touches

17 **"Lift" the bangs.** Turn the work so you can do the smooth shading technique. Touch down at the edge of the hair and pull the shading onto the forehead skin. Once the shading is pronounced in that area, do an undercut just where the hair meets the skin.

18 **Add more layers.** Increase the temperature to setting #5 to work behind the ear. Then, add more layers of hair by adding more lines at this darker value. Practice the subtle twist of the wrist to create short hair strokes in this area. I place the most details at the temple and forehead because that is where I am trying to draw the attention of the viewer.

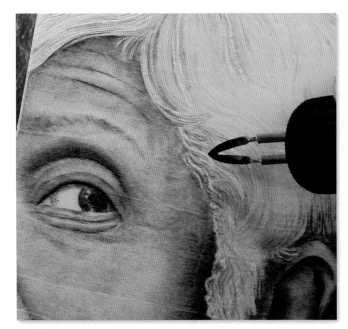

19 **Add depth around the temple.** Increase the temperature to setting #6 and very lightly add more depth to the temple hairs. You can make the hair look thicker by lightly placing these darkest areas into the mix. Add more depth in the hair around the ear and behind.

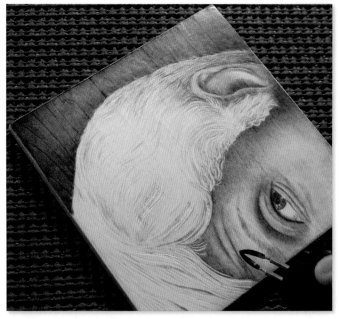

20 **Shade the skin again.** Reduce the heat to setting #4 and add another layer of shading to the skin, blending from the hairline and pulling the shading toward the nose. Erase multiple times to assure no graphite is left visible.

HAIR VARIATIONS

Facial Hair

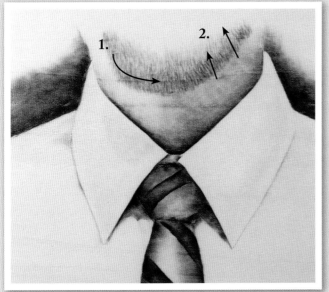

Hair is hair, so you will work facial hair the same way you do any other kind. My son-in-law Casey has whiskers that are medium thick and a lighter shade. To burn them, I smudge the chin/jaw area to define it (arrow 1). Then, working upside down, I touch down at the bottom of each hair and pull toward the mouth (arrow 2). The directional arrows you trace when you first set up a portrait help you know which direction the hair is growing. Casey's chin hair is short, so I made short strokes, lifting at the end to create the lighter and thinner area under his lip.

Ponytail

I used the smudge technique (see page 84) to create a ponytail. I used a higher temperature to create a darker color and burned in slow, long strokes to mimic the hair being pulled back into the ponytail. Build a ponytail by starting at the crown and pulling toward the back of the head, and then starting at the ponytail area and pulling back around to the side and crown.

Curly Hair

For curly hair, burn in layers. First, smudge and smooth shade the wood where the hair will be, leaving it a couple of shades lighter than usual so the dark curls will show. Then, I use a 1.5mm ballpoint tip to draw S-shaped curlicues. (You can use any comparable nib that allows you to swirl.) Draw smaller curlicues for tighter curls and larger ones for looser curls. When you are satisfied with the curls, smudge the skin where the hairline begins.

Short, Fine Hair

This little girl has short, fine hair that was combed forward to create bangs. I shaded in the shape of her head and then burned individual hairs to fill in. Her hair is thicker on the left side. I used a lower heat setting and long, slow strokes to make the detailed hairs. Notice the undercut that lifts the bangs from her forehead and the smudged lines for eyebrows.

Straight Long Hair with a Part

There are numerous ways to burn hair. This is one easy way. I'll begin with a large smudge to show what can happen with more layers on top of it. This smudge could also be referred to as a burnish; either way you are flattening the wood fibers.

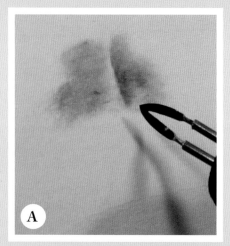

A

Burn two smudges. Use temperature setting #4. Pretend this is the top of someone's head and make two smudges side by side. Leave an unburned area for the center part. We'll detail the smudge on the right.

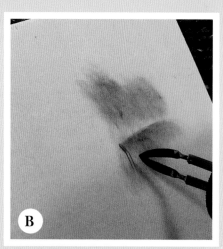

B

Darken the area along the part. Use the smooth shading stroke to touch down at the center part and pull to the right.

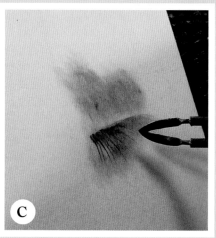

C

Burn individual hairs. Use Angle 1 and slowly burn individual hairs. Space them closer together at the front and spread them farther apart as you move back. Arch the hairs slightly to create the appearance of lift. Use a stroke like the top of a 3.

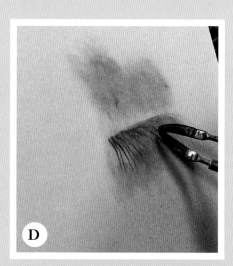

D

Add another layer. Use Angle 3 to blend the solid-line hairs into the surrounding value.

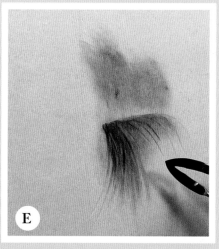

E

Lengthen the hairs. Vary the nib angles to create thick and thin areas.

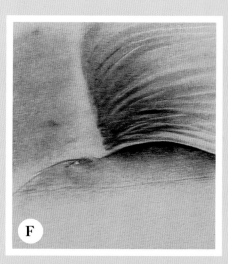

F

Burnish the skin in the forehead area. Do an undercut to add more shading to the underside of the hair, which creates lift.

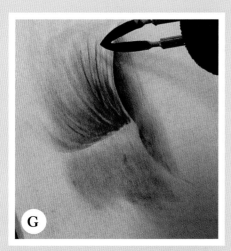

G

Add more hairs. Turn the work so you can lightly touch down and draw individual hairs back to the center part. Do a moving stroke so as not to create a blob on touchdown. I make an elongated S stroke. Reduce the temperature if you need better control.

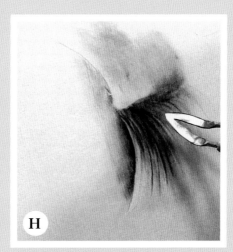

H

Blend the part at the back. Use Angle 4 to smudge together both sides of the part toward the back. Add another layer of shading to the right side to darken the values.

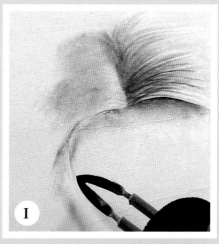

I

Practice leaving a couple of stray hairs. You don't always have to cut them in. You can create them as you go by shading on either side of an unburned area.

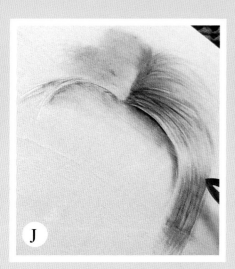

J

Create highlights and movement. Make another smudge with no real edges and lift before merging with the previously detailed hair. Pull shading from the previously detailed area quickly through the new highlighted area to give the effect of hairs. Use Angle 3 to add more layers, always lifting or stopping before crossing over to the upper section of hair, creating a highlighted area. You can keep "growing" hair to any length, flip out the ends or turn them under, or work any hairstyle that is needed.

Clothing

What about the rest of a portrait? It is impossible to keep this book short and cover everything step by step. But by now, you should have the smooth shading technique down. You know how to lift the pen tip to create the visual effect of flat, round, or curved objects. You have made a value guide and a layer guide. Adding details to portraits is simply a matter of applying those basic principles to the rest of the image.

When you're considering your subject's clothes, take a new look at the original photo and compare what you now see with the techniques you have learned. Think of fabric as skin; you will burnish it and add contouring with gentle shadows. To burn the shadows around the neck and collar, you'll use the same technique you did inside a nostril. Wrinkles are wrinkles, whether they are in clothing, skin, or an eyelid crease.

Use what you've already learned to tackle any clothing in the portraits. For this brief tutorial I use a white collar with a striped tie, but the principles are the same for any outfit.

The original photo.

The sepia value guide.

The collar pattern.

The finished burning.

Burning a White Collar

1 Trace the pattern. I cropped the photo to focus on the collar and tie before I made the pattern and sepia value guide. There is no difference in how I traced the pattern. I still used dashed lines where possible to show where the shading goes.

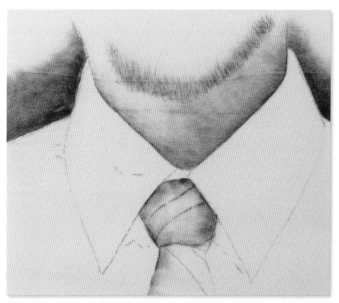

2 Burn the edge of the shirt. To offset anything white, everything else must be darker! I began by burning the background behind the shoulders and collar, and then I did the neck.

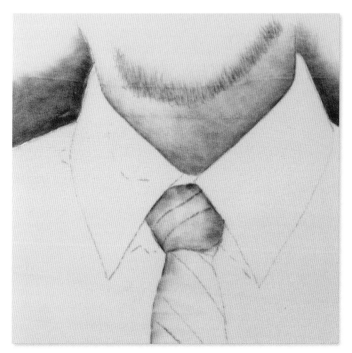

3 Begin the tie. The tie is a round shape, bulging forward. Refer to page 29 for instructions on burning a round shape.

4 Burnish the shirt. Use a very low heat setting to burnish the white shirt and collar. Separate the collar from the shirt with a simple, narrow undercut where they meet. Use Angle 4 to smudge little areas to create the effect of small dips and valleys in the material.

CLOTHING VARIATION

Layered Clothing

A To form the roll of the jacket collar, I turned the sample upside down, touched down at the edge of the jacket collar, and slid the nib toward the center of the collar. Then, I turned the work again to touch down along the bottom of the collar and slide toward the center.

B Create the skin folds on the neck just like an eyelid crease: burn one way using the smooth shading stroke and then turn the work and burn it going the opposite direction. Lower the heat setting to keep the skin fold from appearing too deep.

C Use an undercut to create small shadows under the jacket collar and on the necktie. Turn the heat low to create the undercut on the white shirt and give it the appearance of having clothing folds.

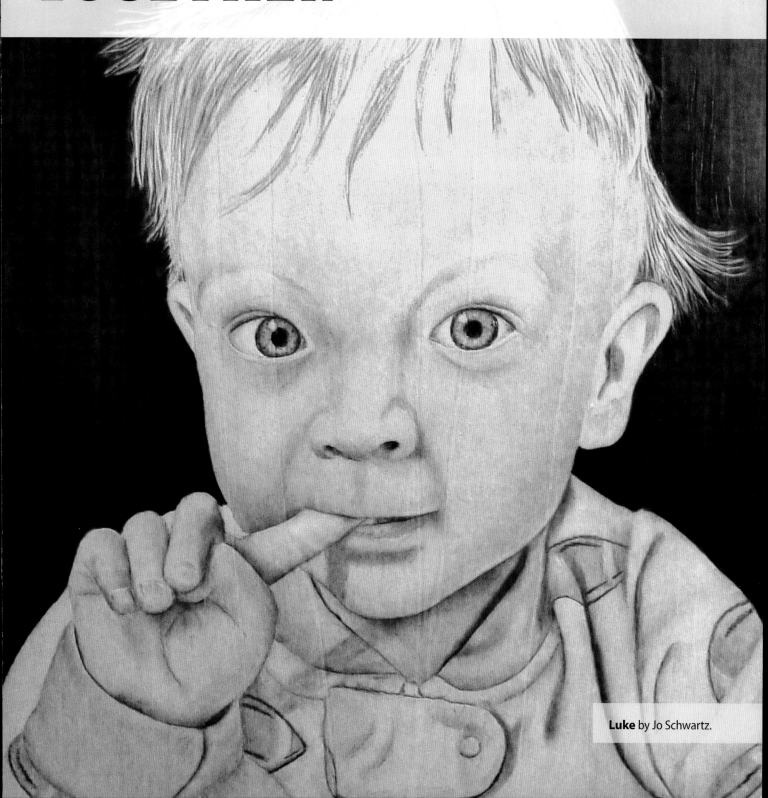

Chapter 5
PUTTING IT ALL TOGETHER

Luke by Jo Schwartz.

Now that you have practiced burning all of the different facial features, it's time to put your skills to work! We're going to put it all together and make a beautiful piece of wood art. To guide you through the process, I'm going to be woodburning a portrait of my grandson Luke. Of course you should choose a photo that is meaningful to you.

It's always best to begin with the eyes. Then we'll go to skin and hair, and then on to the rest of the facial features. Finally, we'll add clothing.

Getting Started

It can be difficult to select a photo. Look at my original photograph. At first glance, sure, it's an adorable baby, but his face is dirty and there is "clutter" in the background that draws your eye away from the subject. This is not a photograph that you want to have enlarged as a color photograph on the mantel.

However, if you crop the photo and darken the background, it becomes a perfect pyrography subject! I especially like the wild hair, which I didn't even notice before I darkened the background. I also smeared out some distracting words on the clothing. I didn't do anything about the food smears on this face—my computer skills aren't that good—but I won't try to duplicate them because it will just end up looking like a mistake!

Once you have selected a photograph, follow the steps in Chapter 3 to edit it as necessary and turn it into a pattern and a sepia-toned value guide. Sand the wood and trace the pattern onto it using a worn piece of graphite paper and a colored pen. I left a 1" (25mm) border around my pattern because I plan to frame the portrait and wanted to leave ample space for the matting and frame.

Portrait: Preparing the Wood

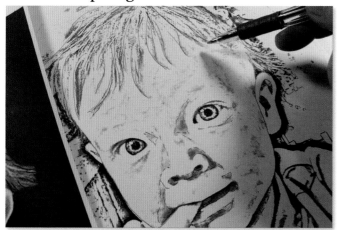

1 Trace the pattern. Use dotted shadow lines wherever you plan to add shading but no actual burned line. Reference the sepia value guide as needed. (See Transferring the Pattern to the Wood, page 47.)

Portrait: Roughing in the face

3 Begin working on the eyes. Use medium-low heat, and test on a scratchboard first. Burnish the area around the eyes and lay down the first layer of values. Pull the shading first up toward the eyebrows and then do a small slide to meet the upper lash line. In addition to burnishing the area around the eyes, I also began to smudge a little under the eyes where I had traced dotted lines. (See Eyes, page 49.)

2 Cut in the highlights (optional). If your subject has light-colored hair like Luke, use a knife, razor, or other tool to cut into the wood before we begin burning. Cut slowly and use several passes to reach a depth that will allow you to burn over the "hairs" and not slip down into the groove. Turn the wood as you cut the areas of hair around the head. (See Cutting in Highlights, page 77)

4 Mark the highlight dots. I located the white highlight dots in both eyes and I'm careful not to burn them. If you accidently burn inside the dot, use a paring knife or razor blade to scrape the burn off. I burned around the iris twice for the sample to get the value. I did not increase the temperature. I know that once I burn the skin darker, I will probably need to return to the eyes and burn another layer or two to keep a visible contrast.

Clean the Nib

When was the last time you cleaned the nib? As you start your new project, make sure there is no buildup on the bottom. (See Cleaning the Nibs, page 19.)

Portrait: Roughing in the Face

5 Burn the nasal areas. I quickly went to the nose and burned those dark nasal areas. I also did a simple burnish and smudge around the nostrils to guide me later where more shading goes. (See Nose, page 56.)

8 Start the background. I'm always anxious to see how the background looks next to the skin. I will turn the wood so I can begin behind Luke's right ear. I will slide from the darkest area into and near the hairs, while also lightly burning between those wild hairs and sliding outward to the darkest background area.

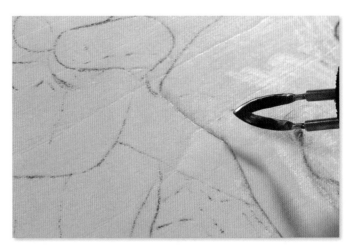

6 Shadow the fingers. I'm burning behind the finger where it touches the cheek. It's similar to burning the hair behind an ear a little darker so it makes the ear appear closer. There is a shadow from the finger onto his lower lip and chin, so I'll smudge that area as a marker for later when I detail the face. (See Smudge, page 33.)

7 Add the mouth. Luke's upper lip is a small arch, which I burned like the eye crease (see page 30). For the lower lip, I touched down on the inside and pulled the shading toward the chin. Then, I touched down inside the mouth where I began the lower lip, but this time did a short stroke toward the upper lip. That darkened inside the mouth. I have to be careful around the little teeth on the bottom. They won't be especially visible, but a hint of a shadow inside the mouth helps the viewer's eye pick that up. If you're burning someone older who has a well-defined philtrum, or who has a mustache, your approach will be different. (See Mouth, page 69.)

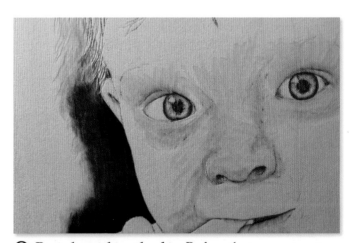

9 Begin burnishing the skin. Reduce the temperature to setting #3 or #4 and begin burnishing the skin on the face (see Burnishing, page 28). Use a light touch. Later you will add more burnished layers that will smooth out the overall effect. Right now it may still look pretty rough and show all of the strokes.

Portrait: Layering the Portrait

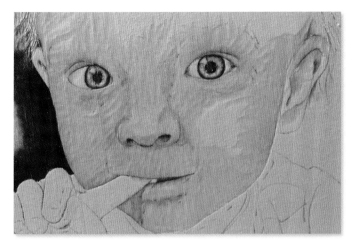

10 **Start the ears.** Sometimes I burn something simply because I am "in the area." While I was burning Luke's cheek, I also began burning the ear folds. Once I had a rough shading completed, I returned to burnishing the rest of the facial skin. (See Ears, page 62.)

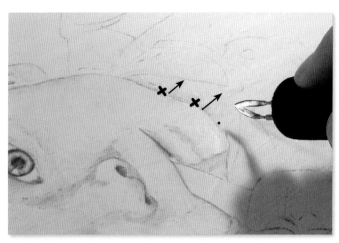

11 **Shade the chin and neck.** I increased the temperature to setting #4 or #5 so I could shade the chin and neck. I touched down at the jawline and slid down toward the chest. The point where you first touch the wood with the nib will be the hottest and burn the darkest. As you slide toward the chest, the heat decreases and the burn lightens. The shading creates a recessed look. (See Chin, page 72.)

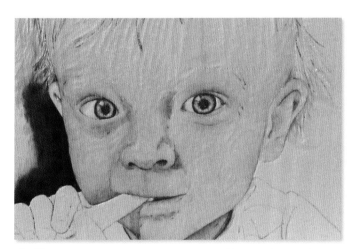

12 **Burnish again.** Begin the second layer of burnishing, using the same medium to low heat setting. Go slow, keeping the strokes light. Smooth the surface while deepening the values. Because Luke has lighter hair, I can burnish his scalp to match the skin so that when I add the layers of hair, it will look more natural. Darken the background.

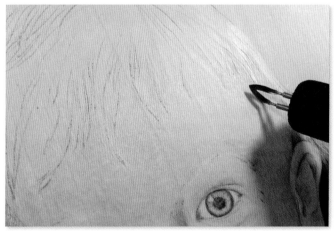

13 **Erase as needed.** In the sample lesson pieces I told you to erase any darkly traced lines to prevent burning dark lines where there should only be shading. I erased any of the traced hair guides that had too much graphite while I was burnishing the forehead area of skin. *(Note: I left the lines a little darker than normal so that they could show up in photographs.)*

Burning a Dark Background

When you're burning a dark background, you can either leave the nib touching the surface and slide around, keeping it at Angle 3 or 4, or make a stroke, lift so the tip can reheat, and then touch again. Practice both; they will create different effects on the wood. Either way, although you can increase the temperature to a medium-high setting, resist the urge to crank the heat higher than that. You are smoothing the wood fibers, so the next layer is easier to burn. I typically burn three layers to achieve the final dark value. Each layer becomes more crisp and shiny. Use a light touch. With the hotter temperature, the wood depresses where you first touch the surface. If you made any unwanted depressions or stroke marks on the first layer, smooth and blend them with each following layer.

Portrait: Burning the Hair

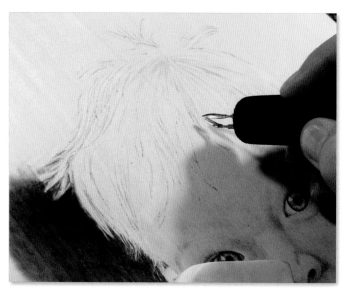

14 **Begin the hair.** I began at the crown of the head, because that is a dark area. I made several passes with a lower temperature so I could look at the photo and try to match the many directions the hair flows. Remember that this is the "sketch" burn (light and simple) to guide you later as you begin detailing the hair. (See Hair, page 76.)

15 **Beware the wisps.** Young children, especially, may have ragged or uneven hair growths, like Luke's bangs. When I traced the pattern, I marked the direction and length of those wispy hairs. Erase the graphite lines just before you work them and lightly burn a few guide hairs to replace what you just erased. Work across the forehead. Then, return to the crown and pull the shading in the appropriate hair direction. This is the first layer, so it should be a rough draft, something to guide you when you begin detailing.

16 **Check the wood fibers.** If fibers from the highlight cuts are standing up, use a fine (220-grit) sandpaper to lightly remove them.

17 **Shade the crown.** Using Angles 2 and 3, gently pull shading of hair from the crown, following the rough hair direction lines.

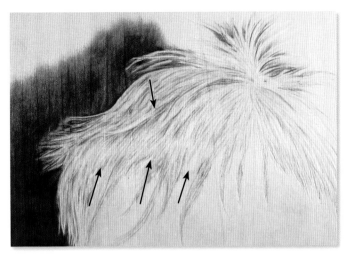

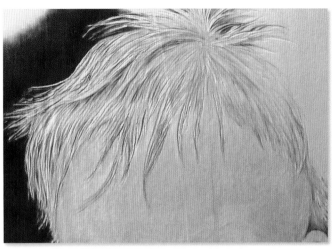

18 **Check the highlights.** A light source circles Luke's upper bang area. To make highlights like those, begin at the crown and pull down toward the area, slowing the stroke to let the wood burn a little darker. Then, lift and float over the highlight area and up off the wood. Turn the piece upside down so you can begin below the highlight, and pull the stroke toward the highlight. Slow down as you near the lift-off area so the hairs are darker. Then, quickly lift over the highlight. When you detail the hair, you can add some very fine and light strokes through that area if needed. You can lightly trace the highlighted areas with a graphite pencil so you know when to lift off the wood, but be sure to erase those lines later!

19 **Layer the hair.** Add three or more layers of hair. Be careful not to burn over the highlights you just created!

Portrait: Burning the Clothing

I am going to begin under the neck and work on the clothing. I will wait to burn the hand until I get a base of shading on the shirt, as it will be lighter than his skin. Although I'm sure your subject's clothes are completely different, the techniques will be very similar no matter what outfit you are depicting.

20 **Create the lifted effect.** Look for areas you know are raised and burn "behind" them to create a lifted effect. I began touching down at the top area of the collar and pulled the shading up toward the chin. Notice the shadow line. I still burn those darkest areas in layers so I can match them in other clothing areas later. Notice how burning behind the snap closure over the zipper makes that area stand out. (See Clothing, page 86.)

Burning Clothing Folds

Working clothing folds is just like working the folds in ears (except much larger and easier to do). They are accomplished in two steps.

Step 1: Knock the heat off the pen tip, quickly set it down at the edge of the fold or crease, slide off to the side, and lift at the end of the stroke. You do not want a hard, solid line at the touch down area.

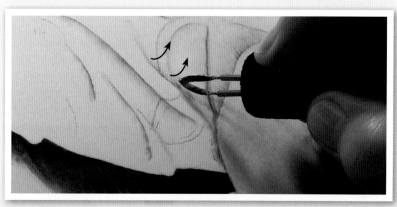

Step 2: Turn the work so you can do the same stroke to the other side of the clothing crease.

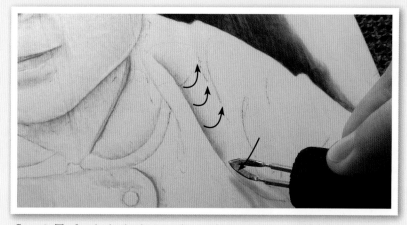

Step 3: To finish the look, turn the work so you can quickly do a "Ffftt" motion (see page 32) to round out the material without adding too much color. Do the same thing on the outside edges of clothing to round it over. With the dark background, it is easy to touch down on the dark areas and quickly "Ffftt."

Portrait: Adding the Hand

Two notes about the hand. First, in most photos, fingernails are not very noticeable. We will only be hinting at their existence, not making a bold outline of each little one. Second, to keep the project simpler, I decided not to add the slobbers on Luke's thumb. If I did want to add them, I would burn around them, just like the highlights in eyes. The more portraits you burn, the easier it will become to do such exact details, but you'll also recognize that sometimes it's best to leave those distracting details out.

21 **Begin with the darkest area.** Keep the original and the sepia value guide nearby as you work. I like to refer to them to see if the shadows are under or over. I began burning in the palm area because it is the lowest, or deepest, portion of his hand. Burning the palm "under" the fingers makes them appear to be above it.

22 **Separate the fingers.** Next I burned a distinguishing area where the middle finger lays on the thumb, ending with shading where the index finger is "under" the thumb.

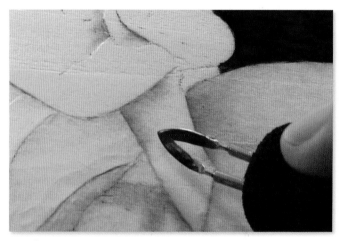

23 **Burn the shadows.** By looking at the original photo I can see that the light source hits the top of the finger, so then the bottom will be the darkest.

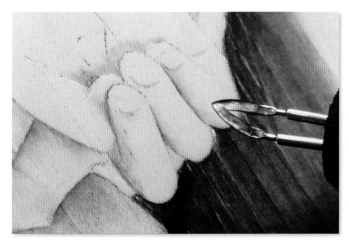

24 **Shade the fingers.** On fingers, sometimes you are simply shading the finger beside it to create the shape! Again, look at the original to see where the shadows are.

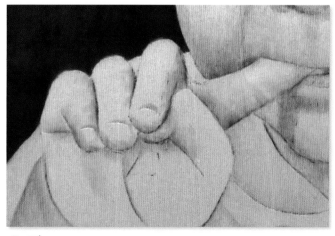

25 **Burnish the skin.** Notice how the fingers were formed only by shading under or over.

Portrait: Finishing the Portrait

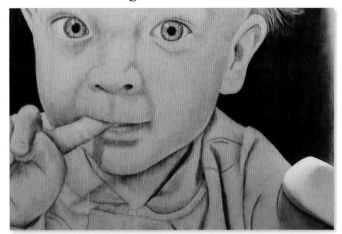

26 **Erase the traced lines.** I usually erase a little throughout the process because I miss small areas, such as inside the ears or along the hairline.

27 **Detail the hair.** Detail where the hair meets the dark background. This is where you will match the dark tone all around the head/hair. Use a hotter temperature to make the wispy hairs more pronounced along the dark background, and use a cooler setting to hint at the fine, light-colored hair on the scalp.

28 **Finish the background.** I left a small border around this portrait. I turned the heat up as I burned around the outside edges, knowing I would be pulling the shading from the outside in toward the hair. That also helps smooth the woood surface, which may be a little bumpy around the hairline as you worked the details.

29 **Done!** This portrait is completed and now ready for framing. See Protecting Your Portraits on page 25 for ideas for finishing your artwork.

Jo's woodburned self-portrait.

Author's Note

I hope that you are also done with your first portrait … and ready to start another one! Once you practice these tutorials, you will be able to "see" that the same details are in every portrait you want to burn. The sample projects let you build your confidence quickly and see how one skill smoothly flows into the next, as you repeat the same movements to achieve different results. You'll also start to notice that you can use the same tips and techniques in everything you burn. A knothole in a tree is burned just like the nostril. Flower petals are shaded into shape like fingers and teeth, never outlined. And, of course, any number of shapes begin with an eyelid crease!

I hope you see how fun and easy burning can be. I would love to see how you are doing. Feel free to e-mail photos of your progress!

Warmest regards,

Jo Schwartz

JoSchwartz101@hotmail.com

www.joschwartz.net

Meet the Author

Jo Schwartz

Jo Schwartz began woodburning in 2005 in an attempt to "fix" a carved character. "It turns out, I can't whittle," she said. "But I did like the look of the burnt areas!" Jo wandered around the web looking for other people who were interested in burned wood, found a site that inspired her, burned some really terrible trees and mountains, switched to human figures, and has never looked back.

Three years later, Jo became the first person to teach woodburning on Antarctica. She was there serving as a shuttle driver for National Science Foundation scientists and support staff at the McMurdo Station on the Ross Ice Shelf, an experience she called, "the most interesting and exhilarating time in her life." Jo noted that because there is no wood on the continent, she had to mail-order wood for projects!

These days, the Kansas native is sticking closer to home. For a number of years, she ran a gallery and studio in historic Old Abilene Town, which is a famed cow town as well as the home of the Dwight D. Eisenhower Library and Museum. She's back to working from a home studio for now, but still enjoys heading into the historic district to photograph the reenactors who roam the area. As a result, she is known for her Western-themed work in addition to her portraiture.

Although she is a fulltime working artist, Jo admits that she has a hard time parting with her work. "Commissioned pieces are easier; they've already been purchased!" she said. "Works of art that I spend so many hours and days and weeks completing must go to a good home, or I won't sell them."

When she's not burning, Jo's interests run to politics. She recently ran for a seat in the Kansas State Legislature. Although she didn't win, she is proud that she tried to make a difference. "It was a great learning experience," she said. "I will always have fond memories and fun stories of the campaign trail!"

And, Jo still loves teaching the art of pyrography. Perhaps due to her own background, her favorite students are woodcarvers who want to learn how to add burned accents to their creations. She is also a regular contributor to *Pyrography* magazine, where she has shared numerous techniques and projects. Regardless of the student or class location, though, she builds their confidence by admitting that her first pieces were "laughable" and then showing what is possible with a little practice, patience, and passion.

About her home studio, Jo said, "My creative zone looks scary, but I know where stuff is! The first shelf has pre-sanded wood, ready to create on, and the shelf underneath has all the different sizes that still need to be sanded. Walking sticks go in the corner. On the right side is the wood from my dumpster diving, along with other odd things made of wood that I want to burn on." Jo stashes her patterns in the filing cabinet and keeps graphite paper, sandpaper, shipping materials, and other odds and ends on shelves in another cabinet.

Jo uses two computer monitors in her home studio. "One is my laptop and the other is used solely to enlarge the subject I'm burning to see details better," she explained. "You can't see the surround sound subwoofer and speakers attached to my little computer that crank out my relaxing New Age music to burn by!"

Jo during her time working and teaching in Antarctica.

Index

Note: Page numbers in **bold** indicate gallery items.